A Life Renewed
1983–1998

Roderick Stackelberg

iUniverse, Inc.
Bloomington

A Life Renewed 1983–1998

iUniverse books may be ordered through booksellers or by contacting:

iUniverse
1663 Liberty Drive
Bloomington, IN 47403
www.iuniverse.com
1-800-Authors (1-800-288-4677)

*Because of the dynamic nature of the Internet, any web addresses or links contained in this
book may have changed since publication and may no longer be valid. The views expressed
in this work are solely those of the author and do not necessarily reflect the views of the
publisher, and the publisher hereby disclaims any responsibility for them.*

*Any people depicted in stock imagery provided by Thinkstock are models,
and such images are being used for illustrative purposes only.*

Certain stock imagery © Thinkstock.

ISBN: 978-1-4759-3037-5 (sc)
ISBN: 978-1-4759-3038-2 (e)
ISBN: 978-1-4759-3039-9 (hc)

Library of Congress Control Number: 2012910036

Printed in the United States of America

iUniverse rev. date: 6/14/2012

CONTENTS

Preface

For this, the third volume of my autobiography I seem to have run out of appropriate epigrams. Let me substitute a verse of Nietzsche's that I have always loved:

Machen wirs gut, so wollen wir schweigen.

Machen wirs schlimm, so wollen wir lachen,

und es immer schlimmer machen.

Schlimmer machen, schlimmer lachen,

bis wir in die Grube steigen.

This verse is particularly hard to translate, because of the dual meaning of the adverb/adjective "*schlimm.*" Literally it means "bad," but it contains a double meaning perhaps best captured by the term "wicked," which can be used in both a pejorative and an appreciative sense. My translation:

If we do well, we'll want to keep quiet.

If we do badly, we'll want to laugh,

And do things worse and worse.

Do things worse, laugh worse and worse,

Till we climb into the grave.

The basic themes I stressed in my prefaces to the first two volumes of my autobiography, *Out of Hitler's Shadow, 1935-1967* (2010) and *Memory and History, 1967-1982* (2011), retain their relevance for this later volume as well. My aspiration to tell the truth about how I experienced the events of my life and to do so in an aesthetically pleasing and readable form has not changed. The title of this volume, *A Life Renewed*, refers both to my marriage to Sally Winkle and the happy product of this union, our son Emmet (born 1991). If a picture is worth a thousand words, then this is certainly the wordiest of my three volumes. The fifteen years covered in this volume were infused with the joys of a happy marriage, a gifted late-born offspring, and some limited but satisfying professional success. This was the "high noon" of my life, before the onset of aging and ill health at the turn of the century.

Once again I owe my greatest debt to Sally and Emmet, whose skeptical but appreciative feedback has kept me from straying too far from my chosen course of honesty about the facts and fairness to the protagonists. Of course, the entire enterprise is suffused with what I hope is not an excessively unhealthy dose of narcissism and solipsism. If it is true that readers enjoy books that their authors have enjoyed writing, then this book should be fun to read.

Spokane, WA
8 May, 2012

Introduction

For those readers who have not read the first two volumes of my memoirs, *Out of Hitler's Shadow* (2010) and *Memory and History* (2011), it might be useful to have a very condensed sketch of their content. This background information might make it easier to identify some of the persons mentioned in this book.

On New Year's Eve 1931 my mother (1912-1998), youngest daughter of Elizabeth LeRoy Emmet (1874-1943) and the financier Nicholas Biddle (1678-1924), married my father Curt Ernst Friedrich von Stackelberg (1910-1994) in Munich where they had met as students of art and of law, respectively. Their marriage produced four children, my siblings Olaf (b. 1932), Betsy (b. 1934), and Tempy (b. 1938), as well as myself (b. 1935), before their relationship ended in divorce at the height of the Second World War in 1942. My mother returned to the U. S. with her four children in 1946, settling in the northwest corner of Connecticut, where we grew up. The first volume of my memoirs covers my life up to age thirty-two in 1967. It was pretty much a wasted youth as I was one of the young people who "dropped out" during much of the 1960s.

Mama had a complicated relationship with her two older siblings, Uncle Nick Biddle (1906-1986), whom she adored, and Aunt Temple Edmonds (1908-1983), with whom she was on a much more competitive footing. The two sisters had to make a real effort just to keep their rivalry from turning into open conflict,

The second volume of my memoirs is about my belated professional success and simultaneous marital failure. My marriage to my first wife Steffi Heuss (b. 1941) in 1965 ended in divorce in 1983. But it did produce two fine offspring, my daughter Katherine ("Trina") born in 1966 and my son Nicholas ("Nick") born in 1971. It is to my grandchildren, Sigugeir ("Siggi") Jonson (b. 2000), Bryndis ("Brynnie") Jonson (b. 2002), and Sebastian ("Sebi") von Stackelberg (b. 2010) that this memoir is primarily addressed.

1

A New Beginning with Sally, 1983–1985

In late October, 1983, I first met Sally Winkle at the home of Olivia Caulliez, still married to my former Gonzaga colleague John Shideler at the time. Sally had just begun teaching German language and literature at Eastern Washington University. We had both attended the annual German Studies Association conference held that year at the University of Wisconsin in Madison, where Sally was completing her PhD in German language and literature. We had not met at the conference, but it gave us plenty to talk about. My visit to Madison had indeed been a memorable occasion for me, my only visit to one of the major sites of the student rebellion and anti-war movement of the 1960s, with which I sympathized so greatly. The balmy weather drew hundreds of students into the streets to enjoy the "Indian summer." The student union, the *Rathskeller*, still served beer at the time, and the atmosphere of the city and especially the campus struck me as marvelously liberal and inviting. For Sally, who had already lived in Madison for six years, the weekend was probably nothing special, but we found in our conversation at Olivia's that we were on the same wavelength in our political views and intellectual interests—so much so that for all practical purposes we were "computer-matched." Sally had been an active member of the graduate teaching assistants' union at the University of Wisconsin and had participated in a strike for higher wages and better working conditions a year or two before. Within a week we became an inseparable couple. Our sixteen-year age difference was no problem, at least not at the time. "It turns me on," Sally told me, "that you think I am young." And I was turned on by her slim figure and excellent mind.

With Sally in 1983

I had been searching for a mate for more than a year, ever since my final separation from Steffi at the end of 1982. I was particularly attracted to two of my young female colleagues at Gonzaga, but they were each other's best friends, and in my clumsy efforts at courtship I only managed to antagonize both of them! When one of them threw a tenure party for the other one in April 1983 and I was one of the few faculty members who were not invited, I knew I had ruined whatever chances I might have had with either of them. In my journal I recorded my reaction to this rebuff:

> The war between the sexes: the effort to grow beyond the natural attraction to the opposite sex. Hence one competes for the superior psychological vantage point that confers autonomy. Make the other side want you more than you want them.—Insight derived from not being invited to [the] tenure party. Nice to have the insight, but wouldn't it have been more fun to have been invited?

I took a mordant view of my motives:

Irony: in students as potential lovers I look for the parent-less, because they are more likely to defy convention (Kaye!). In older women as potential mates I look for those with close ties to their parents because they are more likely to have internalized the conventional goals of marriage and children (besides carrying the genes of longevity). They are less likely to give in to Lesbian temptations.

Obviously, my own inhibitions played a part in my problematic post-divorce relations with women:

It is easy to say, why not call her; the worst that can happen is that she'll say no. For one thing, it isn't the worst. She may say yes and not mean it. But what is even worse is that she says yes and *you* do not mean it. You mean it only *if* she reacts in a certain way. One inhibition, then, is fear of becoming a fraud, of being revealed as a fraud, because your phone call may promise something you can't deliver.

Another inhibiting factor was the note of desperation that I seemed to convey. Martha Chrisman, an attractive young pianist in the music department who in June, 1986, moved to a higher position at Purdue University, gave me some good advice: "You go too fast. You seem desperate. It takes all the romance out of it. A romance needs a little mystery, a little teasing." Martha told her mother that I seemed very lonely. I asked her what her mother's response had been. "She said she thought you'd better get your act together before you go out." But Martha and I were too different ever to have made a harmonious and integrated couple. She was a bit of a born-again Christian who dragged me to Sunday services at a number of churches.

At the Plymouth Congregational Church with Martha. The minister with the ingratiating gestures and self-admiring public speaking style of Bob Carriker. Martha applying the lessons of the sermon to her problems with Fr. Leedale [chair of the music department], who gave her a bad evaluation after a sneak visit to her class: "I'll get him through love," and "I'm going to think of my problems as challenges from now on." About the minister: "He doesn't play it safe like other ministers. He disturbs people. He has the courage to speak of faith and love instead of how to save the world."

Martha was quite aware of our basic incompatibility. Of a romantic rival, a young executive at a local credit union with whom she was going out, she said: "I don't want him, but I want to want him; I want you, but I don't want to want you." To my plaint that she got sexually aroused with me but then transferred it to him, she responded, "Maybe it's the other way round."

Martha in my back yard at Maringo Drive

When I met Sally, my son Nick was quite relieved. He had become quite worried that if my relationship with Martha developed any further, he would have to go to church every Sunday!

Sally

Twelve-year-old Nick was a bit wary of Sally, too, at first, for fear that our relationship was getting too close, as Sally frequently came over for supper. "When I see three pork chops on the counter," he admonished me, "I get really mad." "I should sue you for waste of gas," he said at another time. "Have you and Sally ever thought about how much gas you are wasting when she comes over here?" But when Sally finally moved in with us two years later in September 1985, they got along very well.

Nick

Sally was very much affected by the second wave of the feminist movement, sometimes referred to as the Women's Liberation Movement, reaching its crest in those years. I sympathized with the movement as well for its emphasis on equality, even if it seemed to make courtship more complicated than it had been when I grew up in the 1950s (not that the more rigid gender roles of an earlier era made it any easier for me). Several months before, on May 6, 1983, I had written in my journal:

> Feminism only elevates courtship to a higher level; it does not change its dynamics. If anything, it reinforces the age-old dynamic: men must really be men: must act independently and courageously: must be prepared to court even the formidable new woman: must not sit on their asses: must not be afraid to act just because women, too, are autonomous, career-oriented, and equal. Another way of putting it is that the war between

the sexes did not start with feminism: it only took a more honest, less devious form.

Sally herself was somewhat torn by conflicting emotions, as recorded in my journal on November23, 1983:

Sally telling me how Miles, her bisexual boyfriend, had analyzed her two personalities and called them "Anna Mae" and "Beatrix," respectively. "Anna Mae" wants to be taken care of by a man, "Beatrix" is the liberated independent woman. The United Nations Association meeting in Cheney the day before yesterday had distressed "Beatrix," because Sally had behaved so much like "Anna Mae". Instead of sitting in a comfortable unclaimed armchair (on which we had placed her coat), from where she could have conversed comfortably with other visitors, she sat down in a corner of the sofa next to me. From there she was virtually excluded from the conversation both because I blocked her line of discourse, and she didn't know any of the people there, except [her colleague in government] Ernie Gohlert , who was giving a talk on his trip to Malaysia. Ernie's presence only made her feel more inadequate, since she had, in effect, chosen to retreat behind me.—The question in my mind was, do I force her, by my behavior, into the role of "Anna Mae"? I had thought that her self-doubts had a different source: that "Anna Mae" felt neglected by my lack of a firmer commitment than our present practice of sleeping together on weekends. The fact that it is "Beatrix" who is aggrieved does not entirely reassure me. For "Beatrix" is angry at "Anna Mae" for wanting what "Anna Mae" wants.

Sally herself was not happy with this artificial distinction between the traditionalist "Anna Mae" and the feminist "Beatrix", and by the time I met her she had fully embraced a feminism that explained gender not as biologically given but as a social and cultural construct. This did lead to some animated discussions in which Sally criticized my more traditional views, as recorded on January 22, 1984:

Argument yesterday with Sally: she took issue with my explanation of promiscuity among young male homosexuals, which was that young men between the ages of sixteen and twenty-five have a powerful sex drive for which there is no socially acceptable outlet. Sally objected to this notion, because the powerful male sex drive is sometimes cited as an excuse to meliorate the blame attached to rapists. When I said it was not my intention to provide such an excuse, she nonetheless objected to the notion that men had a more powerful sex drive than women, because that argument could be used to rationalize rape. This frustrated me.: "You deny reality and truth because it is not convenient to the feminist cause."—"What you call reality and truth may not be truth from a different perspective," she responded. "The whole notion of 'objective reality' has been used to perpetuate an androcentric point of view." I tried another tack: "All I'm doing is providing an explanation for male homosexual promiscuity, an explanation designed to counter the biased view that homosexuals are by nature promiscuous. What you are saying about the application of this explanation to rape is irrelevant."—"You are trivializing my argument by calling it irrelevant. It is typical of the male inability or refusal to see any other point of view."—"I, too, object to using the notion of male hyper-sexuality to justify rape," I retorted. "But that doesn't allow me to close my eyes to the truth."—"What may be true for you may not be true for me."—"But your truth has no bearing on the statement I am making. It is an entirely separate issue."—"From my perspective it isn't. Your failure to see and make the connection is precisely the limited vision I challenge."—"If our perception of truth is so different, we will never be able to close the chasm between us."—"All I want you to do is make the effort to see my side and not to trivialize my side by calling it 'irrelevant,' or 'irrational,' or 'subjective,' or 'illogical,' while validating your own side as 'objective.'"

The argument made me acutely aware of how real the conflict between the sexes is, how unbridgeable the chasm may well be. For it seems that what I am being asked to do is no less than to give up my objective view of reality—a view that has served male interests and does not take "subjective" feminine perspectives sufficiently into account. The argument helped me to understand the genealogy of [my ex-wife] Steffi's dictum, "*Sex ist alles* (sex is everything)." For if the interests and perspectives of the sexes are so different, the sexual attraction is ultimately the only sure bond. It also seemed to clarify the origins of the old saw, to wit that women do not think as logically as men. Thus a feminist attack on sexism reinforces a sexist prejudice.

Sally at home

On December 6, 1983, we attended a firebrand talk by the ex-Mormon feminist Sonia Johnson on the theme epitomized by her militant dictum, "To be born female is to be born behind enemy lines." Her most damning indictment of men was her assertion, "They say, 'if you do not meet our demands, we will not love you.'" More valid, in my judgment, was her starkly expressed insight, "Human beings love human beings. They don't love doormats." After the talk I confessed to Sally that I felt thoroughly chastened, to which Sally replied, "good!" But Sally credited me with a "maternal streak:"

"I like it when you warm up my feet, but I don't like it when you tell me how to teach. I don't like it when you seem to do everything that I do better. It does not help my low self-esteem." John Wagner of the philosophy department went so far as to say (as reported to me by Martha): "The only reason women like Rod so much is because he's a feminist."

My seventeen-year-old daughter Trina came home to Spokane at Christmas, 1983, with some very exciting news: she had just been admitted to Harvard on early decision, an admissions practice that Harvard ended a few years later to enlarge its pool of candidates and to equalize the opportunities for low-income and minority groups. At the annual Spokane Harvard Club luncheon between Christmas and New Year's in 1983, Trina announced: "My greatest fear about going to Harvard is that I think of it as so perfect, such a pillar, that I'm afraid this image will crumble when I go there." She needn't have feared disillusionment, however. Indeed she ended up marrying a fellow Harvard graduate, Garth Jonson, in 1995 and remained a resident of Cambridge or Boston from 1984 on. She completed a doctorate at the Harvard School of Public Health in 2006 and continues to conduct research there on epidemiological risk assessment to the present day. In the spring of her senior year at Kent School, however, her rebellious streak surfaced with a few unhappy ramifications. Trina had taken her mother's VW bug (my ex-wife Steffi did not drive) with her to Kent, where she parked it at the home of Olaf's mother-in-law Mrs. Sleighter, as Kent School did not permit its students to have automobiles on campus. However, Trina made the mistake of lending her car to some fellow students who were involved in a minor accident, thus bringing this violation of Kent School's rules against students' use of automobiles to light. Although Trina was allowed to graduate in June, 1984, she had to forfeit all of the many honors and awards she had earned for her scholarly achievements. Fortunately, these disciplinary actions did not affect her admission to Harvard

Trina in 1984

Signs of teen-age rebellion continued at least for a while at Harvard. At Christmas time 1984, Trina came home to Spokane with a blue streak in her hair. This even merited a mention in the "Undergraduate" column of *Harvard Magazine* which noted the presence in the Yard of a freshman girl known simply as "Blue."

Trina at Harvard

Although as a child Trina had been highly critical of her mother's smoking habit, provocatively posting "No Smoking" signs all over the house, now she came home with a carton of cigarettes, which she proceeded to smoke in her upstairs bedroom over the course of her two-week stay.

Aunt Temple died of cancer in Florida on February 24, 1984, the first of her generation of our immediate family (our cousin, Olaf's benefactor Pauline Emmet, had died the year before). Despite her illness Aunt Temple had stopped off to see me in Spokane on her way to her daughter Liz and son-in-law Robie Rosenthal's home in Seattle in July, 1983. Perhaps she anticipated the approaching end of her life, because she brought Christmas presents for my family, as if she sensed that she might not be around to send them at the end of the year.

> She is exemplary in her grittiness, in her strength in the face of old age and ill health, her total lack of self-pity. But it is precisely this hardness, manifested in rather gruff attitudes, opinions, and even language, this determination *not* to let the world get to her, this invulnerability, that makes conversation with her, not a bore, but a chore. I was hoping to get some information and insight into Mama's life in the 1930s. But Aunt Temple could no longer remember when Mama had come to America [on vacations] or for how long. She could not even remember the last year she, Aunt Temple, had been in Germany herself. None of that particularly interested her. To the explanation of Mama's psyche she did contribute the hypothesis that Mama had had things too easy! She should not have been supported as much as she had been by Granny. There is an unconscious economy in Aunt Temple's outlook; all her sensibilities have become mobilized in the fight to assert herself against disease, weakness, self-doubt, loss of will. A courageous old lady, but tedious. It is the same quality that years ago I called "impersonal," though Mama objected and insisted she was "too personal."

Aunt Temple in the 1930s

The co-residence of Aunt Temple and Mama in the house that Aunt Temple had built for Mama in Vermont had not worked out as planned. Each of their increasingly infrequent attempts to live together in harmony had ended acrimoniously. Just who was most to blame for the friction between the two sisters is difficult to determine. Suffice it to say that they got on each other's nerves. Aunt Temple had the means to live elsewhere, and that was the course that she chose, eventually settling in Florida, where Uncle Nick and Aunt Virginia had already made their home several years before. Mama claimed that Aunt Temple had resented her since childhood for usurping her place as the pampered youngest sibling, but I did not trust her self-serving explanation. It seemed to me too obviously a rationalization of Mama's own life-long resentment of her dominant and successful older sister.

In the summer of 1984 I attended a National Endowment for the Humanities (NEH) faculty seminar conducted by the prolific scholar of German literature Sander Gilman at Cornell University on the German *fin de siècle* (1890-1900). I was chosen as a seminar participant for my "expertise" on Houston Stewart Chamberlain, on whom I gave a formal presentation, but the research project I worked on at Cornell was quite different. It was an analysis of the Marxist appraisal and almost unanimous rejection of Nietzsche's philosophy, most famously in Györgi Lukásc's *The Destruction of Reason* (1954). My motivation was to see if Nietzsche's thought, so easily and often misappropriated by right-wing ideologues, could not be made useful for the left. On the basis of my study of *völkisch* ideology and Nietzsche's apostasy after his rejection of Wagnerian nationalism and religiosity in the mid-1870s, I suspected that the affinities between Nietzsche and Marx were greater than conventionally assumed. Certainly Nietzsche's "denazification" was no longer controversial, at least not in the West, especially after the publication of Walter Kaufman's pioneering demolition of the popular caricature of Nietzsche as proto-Nazi. Also contributing to Nietzsche's "denazification" was his wholesale appropriation by post-modernists as the preceptor of their key insight that, in the words of Richard Rorty, "truth is made and not found." While Kaufman had shown the incompatibility of Nietzsche's ideas with *völkisch* ideology, I focused more on "The *Völkisch* Reaction to Nietzschean Thought," the subtitle of an article I published in March 1983 in a journal edited by my counterpart at Washington State University, Bob Grathwohl. Bob had persuaded me to publish my article in his low-circulation journal, entitled *Research Studies*. Somewhat against my better judgment I accepted his invitation, not only as a favor to Bob, but also because I was impatient to see my article in print. My doubts proved all too sound when the journal folded only a few issues later. Bob Grathwohl, who lost his wife to cancer at a much too early age, subsequently moved to Washington, DC, where he took a position with the National Endowment for the Humanities

Bob Grathwohl in 1984

One of my conclusions in the paper I turned in to Sander Gilman in July 1984 was that Nietzsche's main target was *not* the socialism of the left or the ideas of Karl Marx, whose works he only knew through the distorted lens of the renegade Social Democrat Eugen Dühring, whom Nietzsche roundly condemned for his antisemitic views. Instead, Nietzsche's primary target was the very moralism that was routinely mobilized by the religious right (or the "moral majority") to oppose and discredit socialism. But I could not simply close my eyes to the fact that Nietzsche's ideas had indeed proved very useful to the Nazis, whether in distorted form or not. In an oral presentation on "Nietzsche and the Nazis" I tried to account for Nietzsche's link to Nazism, notwithstanding his unqualified condemnation of German nationalism, his contempt for the Wilhelmine *Reich*, and his rejection of Christian as well as racial antisemitism:

> Although Nietzsche was a profound critic of the German idealist tradition that culminated (in corrupted form) in Germanic and *völkisch* ideology, Nietzsche (perhaps inevitably) incorporated precisely those elements of that tradition that made it easily possible to misuse his philosophy and misunderstand his aims. His tendency to view politics as a degrading activity was very characteristic of the German intellectual tradition,

mirroring the lack of democratic participation in German monarchical society. His philosophy could be easily misused for political purposes because it lacked any grounding in social reality. From the Marxist point of view he did not raise the right questions, since he attached absolutely no importance to the class struggle or economic reform. Living very frugally, he didn't need to worry about questions of subsistence, because he enjoyed a small but regular retirement pension after he resigned his university position at Basel—a very small-scale example of the Marxian principle that the ideological superstructure is ultimately determined by the economic base. But one can also put it differently: a man of Nietzsche's integrity could not, in the last analysis, bite the hand that fed him. Nietzsche's failure to provide any social analysis left concepts like "herd animals," "blond beasts," "superman," or "the will to power" to be misused and exploited for the very cause he most detested. His link with the Nazis lies in the anti-materialist and anti-socialist bias that he shared with the conservative "idealists" that he criticized. He dismissed the "social question," i.e., matters of social equality, social justice, and social reform, as trivial—a distraction from really important questions. A cruel dialectic was operative in the fate of Nietzsche's ideas. In the sense that he was himself very much a representative and victim of Germany's undemocratic tradition, he was indeed, I think, an unwitting contributor to the eventual triumph of Nazism in his country.

So great was my obsession to reconcile Nietzsche with Marx that I finally reached the paradoxical conclusion that while Marxists were right to reject Nietzsche's aristocratic and anti-political radicalism, one had to share some of Nietzsche's iconoclasm, integrity, and independence to fully embrace Marx's ideal of equality—at least in the West. In other words, one had to be an adherent of Nietzsche's values in order to become a good Marxist. Sander Gilman suggested that I send my paper to Ernst Behler at the University of Washington, one of the editors of *Nietzsche-Studien*, the journal in which I had published my article, "The Role of Heinrich von Stein in Nietzsche's Emergence as Critic of Wagnerian Idealism and Cultural Nationalism," in 1976. But the editors of *Nietzsche-Studien* objected to such a sweeping "denazification" of a thinker still widely reviled in guilt-ridden post-war Germany for his putative influence on the Nazis. I had to wait until 1989 for my article's publication in a German translation under the title, *"Nietzsche und der Nationalsozialismus,"* in the newly-founded philosophical journal *prima philosophia.*

While I was at the NEH seminar in Ithaca in the summer of 1984, Sally was working hard on completing her dissertation, later published as *Woman as Feminine Bourgeois Ideal.* Occasionally she would call to express her frustration at the slow pace of her progress and to complain that she was stuck and couldn't seem to find a way to go on. I tried to allay her self-doubts, but I was also acutely aware that if I dismissed them as unwarranted, I might well be accused of not taking them (or her) seriously enough. This put me into a bit of a "catch-22" quandary, damned if I didn't take her low estimation of her work or prospects of success s at face value, but even more damned if I did. "You don't realize," she chided me, "that I have always had low self-esteem, which makes me view things more negatively than they really are." My quandary was predictably resolved when Sally finished her dissertation and defended it in Madison with flying colors in October 1984. Her department at Eastern Washington University celebrated her achievement with a festive dinner in November of that year.

At Sally's departmental PhD dinner 1984

In the 1984-1985 academic year I went up for promotion at the earliest opportunity after the mandatory three years in rank. I knew my chances were not good as my book, *Idealism Debased*, had already been used to justify my promotion to Associate Professor in 1981, and I had only produced one article and several papers since then. But I thought that my service as director of the International Studies Program might tip the balance in my favor. Promotion was important to me for financial reasons. At the time there was still no systematic correlation between rank and salary at Gonzaga; that would not come until the administration's belated acceptance of the annual salary survey of the College and University Professional Association (CUPA) as the standard for determining faculty salaries in 1988 after prolonged negotiations with the salary committee of the Faculty Assembly. However, the Gonzaga Summer School did peg its compensation to faculty rank. Promotion would mean several hundred dollars more for each Summer School class I taught, and I was forced to teach as many as I could to cover not only our household expenses but also Trina's tuition at Kent School and Harvard. Despite the generous financial aid she was awarded on the basis of need, she still had to take out a fairly sizable student loan. Again I knew my promotion would be opposed by my colleague Bob Carriker, but I hoped I could prevail, as I had in my struggle for tenure in 1982. That struggle had continued within the department in 1982-1983 and may have prejudiced our young colleague John Shideler's chances for reappointment in spring 1982. Shideler, a Berkeley PhD, had been hired to replace Father Via as the departmental medievalist after Via's transfer to the directorship of the Gonzaga-in-Florence program in 1981. Shideler, whose academic standards may have been excessively rigorous for the kind of students we served, received poor student evaluations in his first semester, but what may have been even more decisive in the department's refusal to reappoint him was the fact that he tended to side with me in departmental disputes. He may have been right on the merits of the specific cases in dispute, but he undoubtedly overestimated the power or influence I wielded in the department—or in the university, for that matter.

John Shideler

At any rate my application for promotion was turned down in spring 1985. My reaction was foolish and impulsive. I resigned my position as director of the International Studies Program, thus further marginalizing my status and giving my departmental rivals exactly what they wanted!

In resigning as director of the International Studies Program, had I cut off my nose to spite my face? It reminded me of a nightmare I had recorded in my journal on September 21, 1983, a month before meeting Sally.

Extraordinary and therapeutic nightmare of giving up my job at Gonzaga. Extraordinary in capturing the psychological nuances: saying goodbye to faculty services [the secretarial pool]—they are incredulous and slightly resentful of my departure, as if it reflected on them. In the outer office (administration?) they are so busy, they hardly take notice of me. Sitting in the waiting room is Ernie Gohlert [director of International Studies at Eastern Washington University], sympathetic, silently solicitous, reflecting in his attitude his conviction that I am behaving like a fool or a madman. I go outside and am overwhelmed by what I have done—and can't even remember the reason why I did it. It must be because I wanted to write?? The only consoling thought is the one I frequently have in less critical situations: good if things go bad, because it forces me to write, since there is nothing else I can do, no other fulfillment. I turn to a nondescript female friend, round-faced, almost like Sandy Raynor [our friend from Vermont], except it's someone closer to me. She does not want me to talk to her, because she is afraid of the emotional burden it will place on her. I compel her, "Look at me," but saying it in a way to reassure her that I wasn't going to ask any favors or cry on her shoulder. "Why did I do such a foolish thing?" I ask, half-knowing that her response will be one of relief that she is not being called upon for any greater donation than perfunctory encouragement.

Origins: seeing Mike Matthis [my colleague in philosophy who had been denied reappointment by his department], laughing to himself on the couch in the faculty lounge at lunch time, making me aware of how much I have neglected him, making me think he must feel like an invisible man.

Mike Matthis, who shared my interest in Nietzsche (though less so in Marx), was my best friend at Gonzaga until his forced departure in August 1984. We played tennis together, enjoyed each other's company, and engaged in long and sometimes disputatious conversations about philosophy and politics. We also shared a lingering disaffection from Gonzaga as a result of the hostility we faced in our respective departments. Mike and his wife Rose "house-sat" for me at my place on Maringo Drive in the summer of 1984, shortly before they left Spokane for the east coast. Mike later returned to his home state of Texas, where today he is a tenured professor of philosophy at Lamar University in Beaumont.

The election of 1984 was another huge disappointment. In retrospect, it seems strange that we could ever have had any expectation of a Mondale victory. Reagan and Bush carried every state in the Union except Mondale's home state of Minnesota and the District of Columbia. But Reagan's tax cuts for corporations and huge increases in defense spending had led to the largest budget deficit in American history in 1982 and a temporary economic recession. This, coupled with his recklessly militant rhetoric against the "Evil Empire" and his plans for a "Star Wars" missile shield undercutting the Anti-

Ballistic Missile Treaty with the Soviet Union, gave us some hope that his presidency would receive the popular rebuff it so richly deserved, unlikely as that prospect may seem in retrospect. There was an air of gloom as our small circle of friends gathered to watch the election results at the home of Ursula Hegi, newly arrived in Spokane to teach in the creative writing department at EWU. Ursula was not only a writer, but also a chess player. She had contacted me before her arrival to inquire about opportunities for joining a chess club in Spokane. I was happy to be able to tell her about our active local club, called the Inland Empire Chess Club at the time, which I had helped to revive from its moribund state several years before.

As champion of the Spokane Chess Club

In August 1985, after Sally spent a couple of months in Germany at a Fulbright seminar similar to the one I attended in 1982, she and I visited her twin sister Sue and her family in Evanston, Wyoming. This gave me a chance to see Sally's parents again. I had already met them in June when they came to Spokane to attend an Elder-Hostel at Whitworth College.

Sally's parents, sister, and niece in Evanston, WY, August 1985

On our trip to Evanston and especially on the way back, we did some sightseeing in the Grand Tetons and Yellowstone National Park. After our return from Wyoming, Sally moved in with us at 9708 E. Maringo Drive. It extended her commute to Cheney to 26 miles each way, often delayed by trains at the railroad crossing on Argonne Avenue until the construction of an overpass a few years later. But living together greatly reinforced the stability of our relationship and worked out well to everyone's satisfaction.

Sally at Christmas 1985

We briefly explored the possibility of moving into a different jointly-owned home, but were somewhat limited in our choices by Nick's desire not to leave West Valley High School, where he had just started his freshman year. The houses for sale in that district were certainly no improvement over our humble and inexpensive abode on the Spokane River at Maringo Drive. There we would remain for another sixteen years, not moving to the South Hill until 2001.

**Bart Bernstein gave a guest lecture at Gonzaga
(with WSU librarian Fred Bohm), 1985**

2

A Productive Period of Scholarship, 1986-1988

In spring semester 1986 I took my first sabbatical leave from Gonzaga University. I traveled to Frankfurt for five weeks in February and March on a German Academic Exchange (DAAD) stipend, leaving Nick, now a freshman at West Valley High School, under Sally's care in Spokane. My research project was on the Frankfurt School of Social Research led by Max Horkheimer (1895-1973) and Theodor Adorno (1903-1969), eventually culminating in an article published in *Dialectical Anthropology* in 1988. By that time I had had more than my fill of reading the works of the many minor exponents of *völkisch* ideology in the nineteenth century and their crazy ideas! The writings of Adorno, Horkheimer, Herbert Marcuse (1898-1979), Walter Benjamin, and many others more loosely affiliated with the "Frankfurt School" were like a breath of fresh air in comparison. My trip to Germany from early February to late March was bracketed by two tragic events, the explosion of the space shuttle *Challenger* on January 28th and the melt-down at the nuclear power plant at Chernobyl in the Soviet Union on April 26th. Mikhail Gorbachow had come to power the previous year, but it was Chernobyl that convinced him to introduce the reforms of *glasnost* (free speech) and *perestroika* (economic restructuring).

There were some unexpected personal losses in our family in these years. Steffi's sister Ulrike died of cancer at age forty-two after refusing all treatment. Her death seemed to give her negative judgment of me that much more force.

Uncle Nick died on January 20th, Mama's birthday, at age seventy-eight. In his last letter to me (prompted by his reading of *Idealism Debased*) he had spoken of suffering from "terminal fatigue." On my return trip from Germany I visited Trina at Harvard, and together with Olaf, who flew in from Cleveland, we drove up in a rental car to visit Mama in Vermont. What sticks in my mind from that visit was Mama's response when asked how she was feeling: "a bit bilious," she answered, with unconcealed pleasure at being able to describe her condition so precisely through the use of an archaic term.

Mama in Vermont 1988

In Frankfurt I was lucky to find a cheap room to rent, thus dispelling my earlier fears that I might be forced to live at Papa's, as articulated in my journal:

> The sinking feeling on learning that no rooms are available in Frankfurt and that I may have to stay in Karlsruhe. Not that I may be bored or may get in the way, but rather that I will not be able to carry out my critical project in that relentlessly positivist and consumerist atmosphere.

I spent most of my time in the Frankfurt University library, where my cousin Eva Ganzlin, Papa's sister Tante Lulli's daughter, tracked me down one day to tell me that Tempy was in town and trying to get in touch with me. He had flown in from London, where he worked for the Kidder, Peabody brokerage firm. He often traveled to the continent to consult with his German clients. As usual, we argued about Thatcher's politics over an excellent meal at one of Frankfurt's finer restaurants. On the weekends I visited Karlsruhe to spend time with Papa and his second family.

With Halinka, 1986

Awarded the *Bundesverdienstkreuz* (federal service cross) for his litigation of cases before the high court of the Federal Republic, Papa had reached the zenith of his career. At age seventy-five he had become a grand seigneur who loved to entertain his guests with excellent vodka, anchovy sakuskas, and fine food and wine, just as in his younger years. He had aged very gracefully, as my sister Stella confirmed when she said, "*Er geniesst es, alt zu sein* (he enjoys being old)."

What accounts for Papa's attractiveness? It's not just the money that permits a sumptuous lifestyle; it's not just a generosity made possible by wealth, it's certainly not his skill or success as a lawyer. There is an element of self-sacrifice, as if Papa had given up the right to lead a normal life in order to act out an existence that gives pleasure to others, even if it is only the pleasure of beholding grandeur, the pleasure of vicariously participating in the last grand gestures.

Papa at the height of his success

Papa at age seventy-five

With my Emmet cousin Leslie Lang in Karlsruhe, 1986

On my 1986 sabbatical I also began work on my book on Nazi Germany, little anticipating that it would be more than twelve years before it finally appeared under the Routledge imprint in spring 1999 as *Hitler's Germany: Origins, Interpretations, Legacies*. On January 8th, 1986, I wrote in my journal:

> My book on the Nazis must surmount the East-West split: it must be written not from one side or the other, but from the higher vantage point that incorporates the best of both points of view.

> Nazism is a *political* topic, not a question of occultism, psychology, ambition, power hunger, historical accident, etc., etc.

Despite (or maybe because of) the accession of Gorbachev to the highest office of the Soviet Union, I was still obsessed with reconciling socialism and liberal democracy. In those days I was often invited by the local media (TV or radio) to comment on international news. Since I taught Russian history at Gonzaga, I was asked to comment on Gorbachev's emergence as Soviet leader. The precise pronunciation of Gorbachev's name had not yet been agreed upon, so I called on Ed Yarwood, who taught Russian at Eastern Washington University, for assistance. He said that there was no particular rule that applied in this instance, so I wrongly put the accent on the second syllable, Gorbáchev, to my later embarrassment. Nonetheless, my periodic TV appearances were successful enough to persuade the local ABC station to invite me to serve as their "expert" commentator for the 1988 presidential election. This was an invitation I felt obligated to decline, not only because of my lack of "expertise" on American electoral politics (which I gave as my excuse), but also because I knew I would never be able to disguise my partisanship for the Democratic Party. I had earlier seriously embarrassed my son Nick, who was watching the news with his friends, by my critical comments on Reagan's cold war policies. "Can't you ever say anything nice" he admonished me, "about our president?" When I tried to explain the reasons for my vehement objections to Reaganism, Nick's response was, "Life is more than just a lecture, Dad."

Nick 1985

Nick 1986

Nick playing ping-pong in the basement, 1987

A sampling of journal entries gives some idea of my evolving political views, ultimately disappointed by the failure of Gorbachev's reforms to bring about a democratic socialism:

> 16 Jan 1986 Liberalism descends into fascism when it is conceived only as freedom for power.

27 Jan The point is this: a "free" society creates the conditions in which strength can exert itself at the expense of the "weak." However, to ensure a system in which the "weak" will not be short-changed or exploited, but in which people will continue to remain "free," people's voluntary assent to the norms of non-exploitation must be gained. In the absence of such voluntary assent, some form of coercion is necessary, leading to the paradox (and confirming the validity of a dialectical interpretation of history) that strong leaders must exert powers that will seem arbitrary and illegitimate to those who do not accept the norms of a socialist society.

4 Feb The mechanism of coercion is more impersonal and better concealed in the West in that no individual or group—no KGB—can be held responsible. That is not the least "genius" of the market from the conservative point of view. Victims of market forces blame natural causes, or bad luck, not the representatives or institutions of the social order, for their misfortune.

9 Apr The American dialectic: the power that this country wields is at least in part a consequence of its attractiveness—the appeal of its civil liberties—to so many people in the world. But the United States is hampered—thank God—in the full exercise of its power by those very same liberal institutions, which can't be done away with—much as the propertied would like to—without destroying the source of American attractiveness and hence some of its power. The conflict has to and will be fought out in America itself. Because as long as America retains its liberal institutions it remains strong—and thus at least potentially capable of much mischief in the world. To wish a reduction of American power is in a sense to wish a diminution of what makes the United States appealing—its liberalism. So the responsibility of taming its power lies with us—its citizens. But in the very act of exercising its liberal democratic institutions, we are strengthening the U. S. and contributing to the power we seek to rein in. Is this what Hegel meant by the cunning of reason, the dialectic of history, and the passage of the "world spirit" from one country to another?

11 Apr Problems of socialism: what do you do when there always seems to be a majority in favor of a system that excludes, or exploits, or handicaps, or penalizes certain minorities (for instance, the poor)?

1 May *Every* system contains the potential for abuse. Liberals claim that their system is best because it recognizes and acknowledges the fallibility of humans. But they thereby enshrine that fallibility!

9 May The positive aspect of Reaganism is that we now know what to fight. Welfare statism puts the left in such a difficult position: on the one hand, it is not nearly equitable enough; on the other hand, we cannot deny our support to ameliorative measures—even if they strengthen a system that is basically inequitable. Reagan eases this uncomfortable choice.

15 May Anti-Marxists want to have it both ways. They argue that "individual initiative" (i.e., the acquisitive drive) is essential to productivity and progress, but they deny that economic motives and relations are fundamental to human activities. But economic activity *always* has social consequences because of its effect on property values, the value of money, hence prices and wages, etc. That is why there must be some sort of social control. Farmers (like Mama), for instance, are victims of economic pressures not of their own making.

21 Nov 1987 The challenge confronting America: is it possible to create a truly inclusive middle-class society (the American dream)? Then there would in fact be no need, no use for Marxism.

4 July 1988 Democratic socialism can only succeed within a consensus on the desirability and legitimacy of a socialist economy. The current turmoil in the USSR attests to how far they have finally come: at last the party feels secure enough about the popularity and viability of socialism to permit open debate. No wonder our conservatives view what is going on with such misgivings!

Little did I anticipate that it was the Soviet bureaucracy itself, filled with ambitious people with no real commitment to Marxism, who would take the lead in the transformation of the Soviet Union into a brutally corrupt capitalist system a year or two later!

Mama's sweater, 1986

The other great interest of my sabbatical semester in spring 1986 was my continuing (but ultimately unavailing) project of reconciling Nietzsche with Marx.

If we perceive the great crimes of our age as the product of a perverted morality, then Nietzsche has something to say to us.

Nietzsche's point?? Christianity is one thing in the minds of the truly humble—Jesus; another thing in the hands of the arrogant and intolerant—Paul. One cannot say Christianity is right or wrong. One can say it is admirable when practiced, an abomination when preached.

[Richard] Rorty's article in the *London Review of Books* invoking Nietzsche in behalf of the adage, "truth is made, not found." Truth is a function of choice of vocabulary, not of more perfect representation of outer reality or more perfect expression of inner reality. The dialectic is evident in that this kind of relativism can serve the communist cause by debunking the absolute claim to truth of religion, etc.; but it is now generally used to invalidate the communist claim of representing the true course and purpose of history. All is contingency. No system is more right than any other—except, of course, the system that acknowledges that truth (namely, liberalism)! To make this angle of attack possible, communism must be portrayed as a secular religion making claims to absolute truth. What gets lost is any appreciation of communism as simply partisanship for the weak and oppressed and the poor, which is exactly what liberals *want* to lose!

Marxism (or true democracy), by balancing the scale in favor of the under-classes and outcasts, by questioning the privileges of the wealthy and powerful, by refusing to accept their superior social positions as givens, provides the necessary challenge that fosters greatness (which can't be defined *a priori*, which develops dialectically). Nietzsche understood this.

Nietzsche's problem is the German problem: no *political* awareness. Hence he generalizes his indictment of a specifically German world view into an attack on a human, or at least "Western" world view: Christianity, morality, etc. It is important, especially for Marxists, to situate Nietzsche's philosophy in the context of his German experience. Nietzsche doesn't help us to understand the world, as Marx does, but he does help us to understand Germans!

New York Review article on "*Volksgeist*" vs. "European culture:" what it fails to take into consideration is the crucial difference between *Volksgeist* as national liberation and as national domination and oppression. What it fails to take into consideration, in other words, is the economic base. It is the economic base that determines victimization or oppression. This neglect is what Marxists rightly impugn. The differing manifestations of *Volksgeist* provide a good illustration of the dialectic: *Volksgeist*, a liberating nationalism, carries within it the seeds of oppression. Nothing is either good or evil, except under certain conditions. Nietzsche's failure to analyze these conditions in political terms is his true weakness.

One thing is undeniably true: Nietzsche has poisoned many minds. Mediocre minds under Nietzsche's influence make mediocrity stronger. Nietzsche doesn't change the quality of minds, he enhances self-confidence. Fascism: the petty bourgeois mind under Nietzsche's influence.

Dostoyevsky's Underground Man—"a person will desire what is injurious to himself simply to have the right to desire for himself even what is very stupid"—and Nietzsche's nihilist, who would rather will nothingness than not willing at all.

Nietzsche so *"aktuell"* (relevant) because his rejection of majoritarianism, which can be used for a critique of *both* socialism and bourgeois democracy. Moreover, his criticism of the old order, of Bismarck and Wilhelm II, but also of idealism and religion, absolves him of being reactionary. He is ultra- (hence post-) modern, futuristic, open-ended— hence his appeal today. What those who want to activate him against socialism alone fail to acknowledge is that he can equally well be activated against liberal democracy. But he can't be dismissed as simply a mouthpiece of the old order, as some Marxists do.

The current Nietzsche renaissance as a desperate search for a philosophically sophisticated alternative to Marxism. But not all negative: it is also a symptom of the kind of urges and motives that inspired Marx, but that cannot express itself in a commitment to Marxism in a system dominated by capital. Nietzsche at least gives one the courage to turn one's back on traditional authority.

But then there are the "tough" Nietzscheans who appreciate his *salutary* critique of liberal democracy, the ruthless unmasking of liberal ideology, not out of any sympathy for fascism, but because the tough Nietzschean attack provides a safeguard *against* fascism. This is quite different from the "gentle Nietzscheans" who portray him as some sort of proto-liberal.

It all depends on why Nietzsche is valued today: is it because his skepticism serves as a useful counterweight against Marxism, or is it because he has diagnosed the nihilism that has led us to the brink of nuclear self-destruction?

Given my scholarly interests, the most important historical controversy of 1986-1987 for me was the dispute known in Germany as the *Historikerstreit*. Precipitated by an article by the historian Ernst Nolte in the leading conservative newspaper *Frankfurter Allgemeine Zeitung* (FAZ) entitled , "*Vergangenheit die nicht vergehen will* (the past that will not go away)," the dispute pitted defenders of the "new conservatism" of the Reagan era against liberal critics of the "new cold war." Nolte called for the same dispassionate analysis of Nazism as all other past events eventually received. Reagan's visit the previous year with West German Chancellor Helmut Kohl to the Bitburg military cemetery that also contained the graves of numerous SS soldiers had already set the tone for the new Cold War hawks who wanted to play down the Nazi past to strengthen West German commitment to the fight against Soviet communism. My comment in my journal was: "Bitburg is the revival of appeasement: even the SS have their uses in the struggle against the Reds." Nolte argued in favor of a more positive reappraisal of Nazism, without denying Nazi extremism or the Holocaust. He interpreted Nazism as an understandable, if excessive (*überschiessende*) reaction of a fearful bourgeoisie to the greater horror and threat of the Russian Bolshevik Revolution. In that way he could even give the Holocaust a rational justification, while incriminating communism for having precipitated the violent fascist reaction. Some of Nolte's defenders, such as Joachim Fest, a biographer of Hitler and editor of the FAZ, went so far as to describe the Holocaust as just another of the tragic catastrophies that have always marked the course of human history. For liberal American historians Nolte's interpretation of fascism as a reaction to and mirror image of the prior and allegedly more lethal communist movement provided an unpleasant provocation, as I tried to point out in several entries in my journal in January 1987:

> The German Historikerstreit: Nolte's analysis of fascism as basically anti-Marxism is correct; his effort to derive a certain justification of fascism from this is not. Nolte *is* performing a useful service in "historicizing" fascism, i. e., embedding it in its historical context and thus facilitating understanding. But his analysis does not so much "relativize" fascism (as just a militant and not totally unwarranted response to communism) as it discredits militant right-wing anti-communism (though of course that is not how Nolte, or his liberal critics, see it). Liberal American critics, such as [Stanford Professor Gordon] Craig [who wrote about the dispute in the *New York Review of Books*] have such problems with Nolte, et al., because they cannot criticize his anti-communism since they share it. So they have to claim (citing [historian Eberhard] Jäckel) that Hitler did not eliminate the Jews out of fear of Bolshevism. They sidestep the *real* issue—the analysis of fascism—to focus on a much narrower topic—the uniqueness of the Holocaust. The typically liberal cop-out of taking

a relentlessly positivistic and empirical approach. What other state, after all, had used gas in so systematic a fashion on men, women, and children? And they reject (or attack) what is strongest about Nolte—his "philosophizing," his dialectic, or, more accurately, phenomenology— rather than his basic values. Nolte provides a real challenge: he is forcing Americans to confront the implications of their anti-communism. They don't like it.

The real issue in the controversy was not the historical interpretation of Nazism but the politics of the new Cold War at the height of the Reagan era:

Nolte's project: in the outrage over fascism and its atrocities, don't lose sight of the prior and perhaps greater atrocities of communism. Precisely because he is aware of the importance of the anti-communist impulse in fascism, he is concerned (as are Fest and the FAZ) that outrage about fascism (and the charge that Nazi crimes are uniquely horrible, execrable) may dim people's anti-communist ardor, may turn the youth of the Federal Republic into guilt-ridden pacifists. None of them are apologists for fascism. All of them *are* Cold Warriors. This is really a debate about motives, not substance. Critics of [Jürgen] Habermas have tried to turn it into a debate about substance—or rather, they have tried to discredit Habermas because he called into question the motives of Nolte and his defenders rather than offering a substantive rebuttal of Nolte's interpretation. The hidden (and not so hidden) agenda of all the participants is present policies and the present political ethos, not history at all. An extremely instructive example of how the interpretation of history is relevant to contemporary politics! American liberal historians have such problems with this controversy because they don't even accept Nolte's analysis of fascism (at least not whole-heartedly). What is at issue is not the interpretation of fascism or the uniqueness of the Holocaust, but the Cold War, the *Wende* (conservative turn). Nolte is well aware that his quite accurate analysis of fascism can work both ways—to indict anti-communism or to "relativize" or "historicize" Nazism. Since he doesn't want the former, he is left with no choice but to pursue the latter. Americans take a cop-out: fascism is not anti-communism (in essence) but unique (demonic) evil.

Ultimately what was at stake for Nolte and his defenders in the *Historikerstreit* was not just German support for the new Cold War, but rejection of the values of the generational revolt of the 1960s in favor of the new conservatism of the 1980s. Hence the title of the article on the *Historikerstreit* I published in *Radical History Review* in 1988: "1986 vs. 1968: The turn to the Right in German Historiography."

Several years earlier Sally and I had become quite active in protesting the Reagan Administration's support for the right wing government of El Salvador, whose paramilitary death squads had assassinated Archbishop Oscar Romero and murdered three American nuns in 1980. Reagan also financed counter-revolutionary terrorists known as "Contras" in their efforts to overthrow the Sandanista government in Nicaragua. Sally had become a member of the steering committee of the Central America Solidarity Association (CASA) cofounded by her young colleagues from the economics department at Eastern Washington University, future Democratic majority leader of the Washington state senate, Lisa Brown, and the later Washington delegate to the Northwest Power Council, Tom Karier. The committee was so successful at raising funds that they could even hire a paid staff, headed by Scott Nicholson. Kevin Baxter was a sports writer for the local daily, the *Spokesman-Review* (today he is on the staff of the *LA Times*). Julie Barnard was the activist daughter of the former mayor of Spokane, Sherry Barnard. Mort Alexander, originally from New York, was part of an organic farming commune called Tolstoy farms.

CASA 1986. Scott Nicholson, Kevin Baxter, Susan Reicheldorfer, Lisa Brown, Sally, Julie Barnard, Mort Alexander, Tom Karier

In 1986 the so-called Iran-Contra scandal burst on to the scene with the disclosure that money from arms sales to Iran had been diverted by the White House to finance Contra attacks against Nicaragua in violation of a law barring U.S. aid to the Contras—a law passed by the Democratic Congress in a futile effort to halt the aggressive policies of the Reagan Administration in Central America.

Protest at the Federal Building, Spokane, in 1986

But those of us hoping that the judicial system would now function as impartially as it had in the Watergate scandal were to be disappointed. None of the persons responsible for the illegal diversion of funds or efforts to cover up the affair ever went to jail. In fact, one of them, Marine Lt. Col. Oliver North, an aide to National Security Adviser John Poindexter, became something of a national hero to conservatives, despite admitting his role in revising, shredding, and removing key documents in the affair. I was able to use the resulting "Olliemania" as a teaching tool in my course on Hitler's Germany.

On January 1st, 1987, at Tom Karier's suggestion, we held the first of our annual New Year's Day "Open House" brunches. We made a mistake, not to be repeated in future years, of not specifying any hours. While most of our guests arrived in the late morning, some, including my Whitworth College colleague Bob Lacerte and his wife, did not arrive until late afternoon.

With Tom Karier and Jill Gibian 1985

Sally with Lisa Brown, New Year's Day brunch, 1987

Sally spent the summer of 1987 in Seattle at an NEH faculty seminar given by University of Washington Professor Ernst Behler.

Sally, 1986

This gave us an opportunity for a number of weekend outings in Seattle and its scenic environs. We spent a particularly memorable weekend on Orkas Island with its well-known hot springs resort, where bathing suits were optional, but not required. I spent most of that summer working on a review of Abraham's book on *The Collapse of the Weimar Republic* for the *German Studies Review*. It was to be counterbalanced by a review by Bob Grathwohl, who took an opposing view on the controversy over the book, but unfortunately he never lived up to his part of the bargain. Pleading lack of time, he failed to submit his review, whereupon the editors forced me to cut down the length of my review by severely curtailing the space they had originally promised.

Christmas 1987

In June 1988 I travelled east to attend Trina's graduation from Harvard. Sally was not able to attend this festive event as her semester did not end until the middle of June. Trina and her boyfriend at the time, her classmate Paddy Spence, had visited us in Spokane over Christmas both in 1986 and 1987. They shared a common interest in tie-dyeing, which they hoped to expand into a business.

Trina and Paddy

Tie-dye Christmas, 1987

Trina's commencement, 1988

Under the influence of her jewelry-crafting mother, Trina had earlier shifted her major field of concentration from history and lit (my field of concentration at Harvard) to the very different field of environmental design. In her working career, however, which already began with a part-time job while she was still at Harvard, she pursued a different line altogether. She became quite skilled in creating computer models of the cancer risks generated by certain kinds of industrial hazardous wastes. This was the burgeoning field of risk management in which she eventually became very successful.

Trina getting her degree in 1988

I tried to give Trina some advice based on my own experience of having delayed my graduate education too long. "I'm not trying to tell you what to do with your life," I told her, "but if you're planning to get a PhD, don't make the same mistake that I did by waiting so long." It was advice that went unheeded. Ironically, it would be exactly eighteen years, the very same number of years between my AB and PhD, before Trina earned her doctorate in epidemiology at the Harvard School of Public Health in 2006!

In the summer of 1988 I attended another NEH faculty seminar under the direction of Robert Wohl at UCLA. The long drive to Los Angeles was my pretext to finally trade in my aging VW van and buy a new car, a Ford Escort, though that decision was not reached without the usual brooding over the implications of such a move. In the end I convinced myself with the help of a little casuistry:

> Trying to decide whether to buy a new car: is it more materialistic to be attached to the old car than to covet a new one? If a car is just a use object, not a fetish, shouldn't one buy a new one as the most efficient, time-effective means of transportation (the old car, because it needs constant tending, is more time-consuming)? At the very least, one should not worry about the money that a new car costs, for isn't it

materialistic *not* to want to trade in money for time and freedom from distraction?!?

My main concern that summer was to prepare for my forthcoming trip to Switzerland, where I was scheduled to give a presentation on Nietzsche and the Nazis at the annual conference in Sils-Maria in October 1988. Sils-Maria was the picturesque alpine village where Nietzsche had lived and worked most summers in the 1880s. Sally joined me in Los Angeles at the end of July, 1988, and together we visited her parents in Phoenix before returning to Spokane via scenic route 1 along the Pacific coast with a stop-over in San Francisco and numerous stops along the Oregon coast.

Sally in San Francisco

Sally on the Oregon coast

3

Making It, 1988-1990

I probably owed my invitation to give a guest lecture on Nietzsche and the Nazis at the annual conference in Sils-Maria in October 1988 to Papa. He had introduced me to Dr. Roemer, the chief librarian at the public library in Karlsruhe, who had a summer home in the Engadine Valley in Switzerland and was a member of the foundation funding the maintenance of the "Nietzsche-Haus" in Sils-Maria as well as the annual conference at that site. It was Roemer who suggested me as a speaker to the organizing committee of the annual conference. The fact that Papa was a major contributor to Dr. Roemer's favorite causes could not have been entirely irrelevant. On August 11th, 1988, I wrote in my journal:

> The "pilgrimage" to Sils-Maria: at least two ways of looking at it. On the one hand, it seems to perfectly illustrate Nietzsche's insight that the (his) greatest achievements were unplanned. It beautifully caps my long preoccupation with Nietzsche, making all that effort worthwhile. Here is the kind of help from Papa that I do not need to reject, because it doesn't jeopardize my autonomy or integrity. Or does it? That is the other view. Have I come all this way finally to reveal myself as an impostor benefitting from his father's connections? Have I at a crucial moment failed to remain true to myself, to my resolve to make it (or not to make it) on my own, on my merits? It depends on my level of confidence. When it is high, the contingent quality of how I got to Sils-Maria seems like the smile of fortune, a fated event, the confirmation that I have led my life right, the reward for my long years of integrity.

When it is low it feels like I have slipped into opportunism, as if I were conning my way to Sils-Maria in a way that deserves to be punished by my unmasking as a fraud.

Another way of putting it: If my previous refusals to accept Papa's help stem from fear of failure, of disappointing his expectations, does my willingness to accept this help signify a new confidence, a recognition that now I am ready, that now I won't fail, or is it the aberration, the lapse from integrity, that will prove that my fears have been all-too-well grounded?

I was quite nervous while preparing for this high-profile assignment, recording the following insight in my journal in August:

Life is a series of challenges, each of which successively feels like the greatest challenge one has ever faced and each of which later come to be seen as minor hurdles.

So it was in this case. My presentation was a great success, as immediately reported by phone to Papa by Dr. Roemer. I shared the stage with Wolfgang Müller-Lauter, perhaps the foremost Nietzsche scholar in Germany at the time, and later a fellow-contributor to the collection, *Nietzsche, Godfather of Fascism?* (Princeton University Press, 2002). Müller-Lauter, one of the editors of *Nietzsche-Studien*, the leading journal in the field, asked me to submit my manuscript to that prestigious journal, but one of his co-editors felt the time was not yet ripe in Germany for such a sweeping denazification of a philosopher still reviled for his attack on Christianity (and in the case of East Germany, his attack on socialism). To me it seemed clear that for his West German critics, at least, Nietzsche served as a convenient scapegoat to cover up the embarrassing fact that so many German Christians had not only supported Nazism, but had played a leading role in Hitler's rise to power.

In Sils-Maria, October 1988

Sils-Maria

Returning to Karlsruhe from my Swiss excursion, I arrived just in time for my sister Stella's forty-fifth birthday celebration. It was, as usual in Karlsruhe, an occasion for a culinary feast with plentiful libations of excellent Russian vodka and fine German wines. The news of my well-received presentation in Sils-Maria had preceded me, and Papa made indirect reference to my talk in his customary *Tischrede* (dinner speech), in which he addressed his sons and daughters: *"Wenn ihr Erfolg habt, das gibt auch mir Kraft* (when you have success it gives me strength, too)."

With Stella and Sylvia

My three sisters, half playfully, wanted to hear the Nietzschean perspective on the Stackelberg family and our extravagant revelries. Perhaps they expected a Nietzschean stamp of approval for such splendid Dionysian excess. I didn't rise to the occasion at the time, but later gave the question some thought. In my journal I recorded *die nicht gehaltene Rede* (the speech not given). Loosely paraphrased, I would have liked to have said something like this: Papa has emphasized the harmony in our family. I would like to emphasize its variety. All of us have something to offer, but it's not the same thing. Therefore let us show forbearance toward each other. Then came one of my favorite Nietzsche quotes: *"Denn eines schickt sich durchaus nicht für zweie* (for *one* thing absolutely will not do for *two* [persons])." What could I say on the subject of Nietzsche and the Stackelbergs? That only striving for material goods could not be the purpose of life—this belief I shared with Nietzsche, but a birthday celebration did not seem the appropriate venue for such a confession. "Money and property are means and not ends" was a silly platitude.

With Papa and Susanne, October 1988

Of course I was glad that I had not given this rather sanctimonious response to Papa's wonderfully amicable *Tischrede*, even if it did reflect my personal views. At the UCLA seminar with Robert Wohl the previous summer, "consumerism" had been a hot topic of discussion. The term had never meant much to me beyond designating an activity—buying what we need or want—in which all of us necessarily engage. After the seminar I began to understand how it could constitute an ideology and a way of life: consumption as fulfillment and as a diversion from engagement in politics, the realm in which all the important decisions affecting our lives are made. Later, in my journal, I tried to analyze

the socializing function of consumerism: when I go into the Home Club [a now defunct " big-box" store] and look at the bathroom "vanities" (marvelous use of the word!), the thought of having written a letter to the editor protesting the American invasion of Panama [under President George H. W. Bush in December 1989] strikes me as absurd and embarrassing. How could I get so upset when life is so bountiful and pleasant? And furthermore, wasn't I trying to have my cake and eat it, too, by indulging in moral posturing while enjoying the benefits of the policies I was protesting? And I end by feeling that by buying a new bathroom vanity I compromise my integrity—which is probably a good sign, because I could just stop writing letters to the editor.

Consumerism, or its absence, was probably the greatest difference between Papa's and Mama's lifestyles. 1989 was to be the year that Sally would first meet both of them. "I'll be nervous when I meet your father," Sally said presciently; "you'll be nervous when I meet your mother." We left Spokane by car in the second week of June, driving to Minneapolis, where we stayed with Sally's friend from Madison days, Beverly and her husband Michael. From Minneapolis I flew to Germany for a two-week Stackelberg family excursion to Estonia on the 125th anniversary of the founding of the family association in 1864. Our main stop was in the Estonian capital of Tallinn, known to my Baltic German ancestors as Reval.

View of Tallinn from our hotel window

Papa under Lenin's picture in Tallinn, June 1989

Among the participants in our trip to Estonia was the widow of the German war hero Colonel Klaus von Stauffenberg, who led the failed military revolt against Hitler on July 20th, 1944. His wife Nina's mother was born a Stackelberg. Her youngest son Heimeran also accompanied us on our trip.

Papa with Nina Stauffenberg in Tallinn, 1989

Our old estate at Hallinap was in relatively good shape, having been converted to a *kolchos* (collective farm), still in use in these final years of the declining Soviet Union.

Hallinap in 1989

View of the garden from the attic at Hallinap

Röal, the estate on which our father was born, was in very poor condition, having been used as a pigsty during the Soviet period.

Röal in 1989

Meanwhile Sally drove my car from Minneapolis on to Boston, leaving it with Trina before joining me in Germany at the end of June 1989. Among other destinations, we traveled to Bavaria, visiting my wartime home in Ried and at the Elmhof, before visiting relatives in Garmisch-Partenkirchen. Old Frau Neuner, with whom we had shared a house during the war, was still alive and remembered us Stackelbergs well. It was my first trip back to Ried since the early 1960s, when Sweety Degenfeld had taken me through Ried on our way to Hinterhör after Tempy's wedding in Bad Nauheim.

Monastary at Benediktbeuern with the Benediktenwand

I had hoped to scale the *Benediktenwand* in the summer of 1989, the mountain we had so often ascended in our childhood, but the weather didn't cooperate. Instead we spent several days holed up in what had been *Lautenbacher's* restaurant during the war, but now was a comfortable motel, with easy access to the Franz Mark museum in nearby Kochel. Frau Neuner laughed. "*Damals hat man in Sindelfingen über die blauen Pferde nur gelacht* (at the time people only laughed at the Blue Horses). Today they are considered great art. At the time he wasn't popular at all. Today streets are named after him."

Blaues Pferd

On our return we visited Mama in Vermont, with side trips to Burke Mountain and the Shelburne Museum in Burlington.

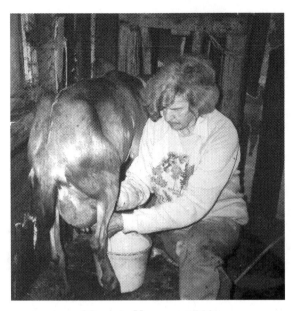

Mama in Vermont, 1989

On the drive back to Spokane we stopped to see Olaf and Cora in Kent, Ohio, before heading back across the Great Plains as I had done so often in the past. This time, however we also stopped off at Glacier National Park in Montana.

In the late 1980s Allan Bloom's (1930-1992) *The Closing of the American Mind* (1987) was all the rage among conservatives. At Gonzaga one of its predictable champions was my colleague, the political scientist Mike Leiserson, whose ingrained conservatism I had underestimated for years, to the extent of referring my friends from CASA (the Central American Solidarity Committee) to Leiserson, who taught a course on constitutional law, for help and advice when they faced legal troubles for civil disobedience.

I am liberated by knowing where Mike Leiserson stands. Only now I can appreciate how *"befangen"* (inhibited?) I was by the assumption that Mike was on our side.

CASA, 1990

Less predictably, the Academic Vice President, Fr. Peter Ely, was also a fan of Bloom's book, although that should not have surprised me, as he, too, had made a shift to the political right in the Reagan years. I remember the interview he gave in the *Spokesman-Review* in the early 1980s, when he in effect welcomed the recession for bringing people back to "the Lord"! I needed to read the book, if only to see what all the fuss was about. Bloom predictably attacked leftist professors, but his attack was somewhat tempered by a countervailing urge to dismiss Marxism as an outdated and irrelevant doctrine. Instead, his book was more specifically aimed at post-modernism, increasingly fashionable in academia in those years and hence the bigger threat to traditional thinking. Nietzsche and Heidegger were his chief targets. Apparently he considered them agents of the left, which was indeed where many self-styled poststructuralists and deconstructionists located themselves on the political spectrum, notwithstanding their conspicuous rejection of the "logocentric" Enlightenment tradition of rationality or any kind of political activism, for that matter. Bloom was a disciple of the philosopher Leo Strauss (1899-1973), who believed that Plato and the other Greek seers had written their works in a code only decipherable by and comprehensible to an educated ruling elite. Bloom, who like Strauss taught at the University of Chicago, did not go quite so far in his opposition to democracy, but he did believe that the new cult of post-modernism was closing the American mind to absolute truths. My reaction:

> The paradoxically exhilarating effect of reading Bloom's monstrous attacks on Nietzsche and Marx: He is so obviously wrong that the effect of his attacks is to confirm how right [Nietzsche and Marx] are!

> Bloom unwittingly attesting to the validity and pervasiveness of relativism in the use of his title: *The Closing of the American Mind.* The need to provide alternatives—the alternative supposedly lacking is the "aristocratic" one—is itself an argument of "relativism." According to Bloom the American mind is closing to the eternal verities, the truths contained in the great books. What he really wants to do *is* close American minds to any alternatives to the authoritarian one he propounds, but given the validity and attractiveness of a relativism and democracy that even he can't deny, he couches his argument in relativist language [the language of competing alternatives].

1989 was, of course, the year that the Berlin Wall came down, East European regimes were toppled in a series of popular revolts, and Mikhail Gorbachev plowed ahead in his futile efforts to reform and stabilize the Soviet system in Russia. In November 1988 I had gotten some hint of the turmoil ahead when I was asked to participate in a panel discussion at Gonzaga with Pavel Kuznetsov, head of Radio Moscow broadcasts to the US (and Chris Peck, one of the editors of the *Spokesman-Review*):

> Soviet official sounding very much like a defector in his criticisms and denunciations of the Soviet system. A strategy to ingratiate himself with the American public, or "genuine" cynicism? In either case, most unattractive. It helped me to understand what dissidents mean when they say that the Soviet bureaucracy is not truly socialist.

Just as you can't have a successful republic without republicans or a functioning democracy without democrats (people who believe in democracy), you can't have socialism without socialists! But I hadn't given up hope. On Veterans' Day 1989 I wrote:

> The breakdown of communism as the perfect opportunity for a democratic socialism. Judging by "really existing socialism," what people resent is not socialism as such, but the obligation, the pressure, to

accept officially propagated doctrines. The resistance is similar to the hostility that any kind of effort at intellectual domination—thought control—elicits, for instance the imposition of religious dogmas or mandatory patriotism.

It seems that at least now we have to grant that the communists did have good reason to be afraid of the "idea" of freedom!

Of course, I couldn't close my eyes to the corruption of communism in practice:

What communism has accomplished: a greater concern for the interests of the disadvantaged, excluded, and oppressed. By the nature of things, regimes dedicated to representing the *weaker* elements in society against the naturally stronger will be dictatorial. This circumstance provides great opportunity for the abuse of power by people for whom the exercise of power becomes an end in itself.

Sally and I followed the upheavals in Eastern Europe with very mixed emotions. On the one hand we hoped the collapse of the East European regimes would lead to a socialist form of democracy; on the other hand, they resembled a counterrevolution by the opponents of any form of socialism more than a successful revolution. They were certainly celebrated as cold war victories in the West. I tried to remain optimistic, but it was hard, as attested by this journal entry in January 1990:

What's going on in Eastern Europe, especially the Soviet Union, may be viewed as an effort to develop a socialist system whose mechanisms of socialization are "natural," not manifestly coercive. A system in which people will voluntarily adopt socialist values; a society in which the institutions will automatically or unconsciously reward socialist behavior and exclude anti-socialist ideas as out-of-bounds, "extremist," "unrepresentative," "radical." It takes tremendous confidence to undertake such an experiment. The "people" are finally to be involved in the establishment of socialism. The risk is, of course, that the people will establish something quite different.

The crucial question, it seemed to me, was whether "Gorbachev's reforms [are] a loss of confidence in socialism or a sign of confidence."

How Gorbachev represents confidence in socialism: he has deliberately relinquished control and granted autonomy to individual agents—while not relinquishing the goals of socialism, a decent life for all, the kind of society that capitalism has never yet produced. He is taking great risks. Those who suspect Gorbachev of cunning and chicanery are really afraid of the new power the ideal of socialism may develop in a context of political freedom.

This led me to ponder

why it is so difficult to predict the future on the basis of history (aside from its dialectical quality—i.e., we know contradictions, even unexpected ones, will develop): history is concerned with motives that explain retrospectively and do not provide a basis for future behavior. Conscious recognition of unconscious motives transforms (or may transform) what was habitual into controllable behavior. Thus previous unconscious behavior cannot be used as a basis for prediction.

In my mind I was hatching a project that I never completed, or even properly pursued:

Book on the 20th century: rise of the masses, yes, but events can't be simplistically blamed on the masses. Rather, it is elite attempts to channel and use mass energies that are to blame for the wars. The right-left conflict does provide the overall framework for understanding the century. Gorbachev as figure on the left and symbol of transition on left—from class-based politics to humanist-ecological perspective. Revolt of minorities not as revolt of the underclass but seizing of opportunities by would-be dominant elites.

While the prospects of socialism were steadily declining across the world in 1989-1990, in our professional lives Sally and I were enjoying increasing success. Sally, who had published her dissertation as a book, was tenured and promoted at Eastern Washington University, while I was finally promoted to professorial rank, which now also included a sizable boost in pay. For the first time in my life I no longer had any financial worries. I was also elected president of the Faculty Assembly and in May 1990 received the Burlington Northern Scholar-of-the-Year award. At age fifty-five it seemed as if I had reached the pinnacle of my career. I was somewhat nonplussed by my change in outlook:

For many years I could not conceive of success as a serious option: it seemed an exception, a rarity, not the norm. Now it is difficult for me to take failure seriously.

We continued our practice of annual New Year's Day brunches with a variety of guests, including John Weaver, who had first drawn my attention at a large Central America Solidarity meeting in the early 1980s. Tom Karier had welcomed everyone "from seven to seventy."—"Seventy-three," John Weaver shouted from the audience. Other regulars were our friends Mike and Gail Gurian, my former colleague and Olivia Caulliez' ex-husband John Shideler

John Weaver in conversation with Tom Karier, brunch 1989

Sally with David Brookbank and John Weaver, spring 1989

Mike Gurian and John Shideler, brunch 1989

Meanwhile, Nick had graduated from West Valley High School in June 1989 and after a summer in Irasburg was off to college at the University of Washington in the fall.

Nick's seventeenth birthday, November 1ˢᵗ, 1988

Having failed to pre-register, he was forced to scramble for the few open classes that remained. I returned from Seattle with a new appreciation for Gonzaga University.

> Reflections on Nick finding all the classes he needs closed at the University of Washington. How heartless and callous this intellectually vibrant, overcrowded, ruthlessly competitive campus can be. Returning to Gonzaga and appreciating the peacefulness, slow pace, and underpopulation of the campus. This is an elite education we are offering: not necessarily intellectually more stimulating or challenging, but an education in isolation from the masses. It is to the University of Washington as the country club is to the airport or factory. It is the right to learn without being pushed and shoved and beaten out. The right or privilege not to have to stand in line. The College Handbook certainly has it right: "less competitive." Almost idyllic, in fact.

In November 1989 the full consequences of US support for right-wing state terror in Central America became apparent. A death squad of the Salvadoran military invaded the campus of the Jesuit university in San Salvador and murdered six priests, their cook, and her sixteen-year-old daughter in cold-blooded execution style. As president of the Faculty Assembly I gave the main address at the packed memorial service in the Gonzaga Student Chapel. But for those of us who had hoped that this monstrous atrocity would finally bring about a change in American policy, the months that followed would prove disappointing. The election of Reagan's vice president, George W. H. Bush, in 1988 had left Reagan's imperialistic policies essentially unchanged, although no one at the time could have foreseen that they would not only be continued, but would even be intensified in the twenty-first century.

March against racism in Coeur d'Alene. Front page of the *Gonzaga Bulletin*

4
Years of Momentous Change, 1990-1991

In April 1990 a distant Stackelberg cousin from Holland, Innet Ehrnrooth, whom I had gotten to know on our trip to Estonia the previous year, came to visit us in Spokane.

Innet Ehrnrooth in Spokane, April 1990

At Patsy Clark's, April 1990

In the pasture, April 1990

Papa's 80th birthday in May 1990 was a multi-day celebration. Betsy was the only one of his eight children who was absent (she had visited him a few years before), and fifteen of his grandchildren (eight of them American) were present as well. Spirits were high, augmented by numerous bottles of vodka and wine. In a humorous welcoming speech, delivered partly in English and partly in German, Papa expressed his astonishment at the number and variety of his offspring, reminding us of the old Baltic saying that the Stackelbergs were more than a family: they were a tribe. At midnight on May 24th the birthday cake was brought in, and Papa managed to extinguish all 81 candles with one blow! The official reception was held in the Great Hall of the Karlsburg, the former palace of the ruling margrave. More than 200 guests came to celebrate and offer their congratulations. The occasion also commemorated the fifty-fifth anniversary of Papa's admission to the legal profession in 1935 and the fortieth anniversary of his admission to the chamber of attorneys at the *Bundesgerichtshof*, the Federal Supreme Court, in 1950.

Papa with Trina on his birthday, May 24ᵗʰ, 1990

At dinner, May 1990

A few days later, at Herr Roemer's invitation, I gave a talk, *"Ein Blick zurück auf den Historikerstreit* (A Look Back at the Historians' Dispute)," later published as a pamphlet in a series of public lectures sponsored by the Karlsruhe Public Library. It was followed by another reception in honor of Papa's achievements.

Papa at Karlsruhe Library reception, May 1990

Reception, May 1990

1990 was a momentous year in world politics. Elections in the now easily accessible German Democratic Republic in March resulted in a decisive victory for pro-Western parties. West German Chancellor Helmut Kohl seized the chance to take control and make sure that there would be no independence for the East. On July 1ˢᵗ the West German currency, the *Deutsche Mark*, became the official nationwide currency. The East German *Volkskammer* voted to join the Federal Republic under the West German constitution, ignoring East German dissidents who favored a constitutional convention to reconcile the two very different social and economic systems in East and West. The four victor powers of the Second World War, including, to many people's surprise, the soon-to-be-defunct Soviet Union, gave up their sovereignty over Berlin. German reunification officially went into effect on October 3ʳᵈ, 1990.

Sally and I made an extensive tour of East Germany in June, shortly before the currency union went into effect. People were already hoarding West German Marks in anticipation of the coming currency change, and although some hotels and restaurants had already begun to raise their prices to the Western levels, rooms in private houses were amazingly inexpensive. In Dresden we called a family that had advertised in a local paper and got a room for DM 20 per night, the equivalent of less than $10 at the going exchange rate. Our hosts had to go to work the following morning, so they gave us free run of their home, asking us only to shut the door when we left. We could sense that personal relations were quite different here from those in the West. Sharing and trustfulness seemed to be much more ingrained in social practices in the East. Of course, their hospitality also struck us as hopelessly naïve, aware as we were of how easily they could be taken advantage of. East Germans also had an exaggerated idea of American wealth and power. In Weimar a group gathered around to admire the VW bug we had rented in Frankfurt and asked us whether we had brought it with us across the sea from America.

On the same trip we visited Jena and toured the famous university as well as the handsome villa of the Darwinian naturalist Ernst Haeckel (1834-1919), on whom I was preparing an encyclopedia article at the time. Haeckel taught at Jena for almost half a century. As one of the centers of German Romanticism, Jena offered Sally a number of research opportunities as well. We also visited Erfurt, where Sally had attended an East German-sponsored seminar in the 1970s—which brought us an unexpected and somewhat intimidating late-night visit by two FBI agents to our home on Maringo Drive several years later. The FBI had been alerted to Sally's seminar attendance by the *Staatssicherheitdienst* (STASI) records that fell into their hands after German reunification. We spent several days in Dresden, which I found very changed from my first visit with my colleague at the Hartnackschule, Renate Sami, in 1964. At that time the scars of war were still evident everywhere. Black was the dominant color of the Dresden skyline from the soot that covered most of the surviving buildings. By 1990 most of the soot had been removed and many of the buildings restored, though not yet quite to the elegance and architectural splendor that the city once again enjoys today. Graffiti on the walls seemed to indicate that not everyone was happy about the collapse of the GDR and looming reunification.

Anti-Nazi graffiti in Dresden

Visiting Ingrid in Berlin, 1990

73

On the same trip we also visited my friend and fellow-Nietzsche scholar Uschi Nussbaumer-Benz and her husband Roland at their rustic home near Zurich in Switzerland. I had gotten to know Uschi after my talk in Sils-Maria the previous autumn. She was working on her doctorate in philosophy, eventually completed at the Humboldt University in Berlin, and was of great help to me as well in polishing my German in my talk on the *Historikerstreit* in Karlsruhe. Her husband claimed to be an admirer of Nietzsche's as well, although his admiration seemed to be expressed above all in a taste for luxury goods. That is apparently how he understood Nietzsche's injunction to always strive for the best! He was very proud of his souped-up, super-charged Jaguar, which he seemed to think Nietzsche would have admired and enjoyed.

Uschi Nussbaumer-Benz and her husband Roland, 1990

I had to return to the US on July 1st as I was slated to teach in the summer session of Gonzaga's new doctoral program. In my efforts to establish rigorous academic standards for the new program, I alienated those students who did not expect to be subjected to such intensive study. Many, if not most of my students had full-time jobs and were working on their degrees on the side. One of them, in particular, was commuting to the weekly class from Canada and resented the fact that I insisted on keeping the class for the entire allotted time from 6 to 10 p.m. (with hourly ten-minute breaks). He was probably the one who on his course evaluation labeled me "a Stalinist" (the seminar was on the Soviet Union). The dean of the School of Education, to whom some of the students had no doubt complained, admonished me that it was common practice in the program to give credit for work experience in addition to academic performance. My evaluations were very mixed, with the number of students giving me the highest rating (usually the best students who appreciated my academic rigor) about equal to the number who gave me the lowest. To my surprise, I was asked to give the course again the following summer despite my mixed evaluations, but I declined. That was a mistake, because I was not asked again. Instead, they hired a historian from Whitworth who became a fixture in the summer program for many years. My efforts to alert the administration to the academic weaknesses of the program went unheeded. The dean of the College of Arts and Sciences left no doubt that he felt it was inappropriate for a Gonzaga faculty member to criticize a money-making program, even if it was academically deficient. Years later I was asked to sit on the dissertation committee of one of the doctoral students in the program. Her dissertation on the civil war in Southern Sudan, in which she defended the rebel side, was well done and was eventually published as a book in Uganda.

Sally had remained in Germany in July 1990, conducting research in Heidelberg and taking a side trip to France.

Sally, 1990

Sally in Paris with Olivia Caulliez, 1990

We also made our annual trip back east, visiting Mama and Betsy in Vermont and my Harvard roommate Paul Russell in Boston.

Mama in Vermont, August 1990

Mama doing her chores

Betsy with Naomi and Matthew, 1990

Paul and Deborah Russell, 1990

When Sally returned to Spokane, we cooperated on a talk presenting our findings in the newly liberated German Democratic Republic during our summer travels and giving our analysis of the consequences of German reunification and the future prospects for the new Germany. We gave numerous joint presentations, including quite memorable ones at the Unitarian Church in late summer and, at the invitation of Sally's former colleague at Eastern Washington University, Jill Gibian, at Eastern Oregon University in early fall. For that purpose we spent a weekend in LaGrande, Oregon, where we also had the chance to visit near-by hot springs in the company of Jill and her husband Larry Smith. Sally and I agreed that a more critical perspective on German reunification was needed to balance the cold war triumphalism that characterized most Western accounts of this momentous event. We realized that we might have gone a bit overboard in describing the unacknowledged merits of East German society when one member of our audience asked with genuine curiosity whether we thought that East Germans might opt to revert to a communist regime! In an article published in *In These Times* in January 1991, "Unification from above leaves German left below." I summarized some of our criticism of the top-down process by which German unification had been achieved.

The momentous events on the world stage were paralleled by an equally momentous event in our personal life. 1990 would turn out to be our one and only year of an "empty nest." In December, 1990, at the ages of thirty-nine and fifty-five, respectively, Sally and I (in today's parlance) became pregnant! We had relaxed our precautions some time earlier on the assumption that, if we were ever to have a child together, now was the time. Let's dispense with the cumbersome contraceptives and let fate decide! I have to admit to some embarrassment at fathering another child at an age at which most people were already grandparents or looking forward to becoming grandparents in the near future. However, the enthusiastic reaction of friends and colleagues assuaged my doubts about the propriety of becoming a father again at so advanced an age. Sally attributed her fertility to the awakening of her maternal instincts by our acquisition, a short time before, in September 1990, of two very cute Labrador-mix puppies, Cloudy and Marley.

Cloudy and Marley

Our new puppies

The date of our wedding was March 30, 1991, which turned out to be a precociously warm and sunny spring day, a perfect day for a wedding.

Our wedding day

Wedding party with Sally's sister Sue

Wedding party

The ceremony was to be conducted at our home by the Unitarian minister Linda Wittenberg who assured us that our lack of faith in God was no obstacle at all! This reminded me of John Weaver's observation, delivered in a conspiratorial tone, that a more appropriate name for his church might be "zerotarian"! We wrote the ceremony ourselves, avoiding outlandish vows we were unlikely to keep. Besides Sally's parents, her twin sister Sue, and Trina and Nick (our official witnesses who signed the marriage certificate), we invited about a dozen of our closest personal friends.

Sally's women's group, 1989

Bob Gillis and Deb Harper

Ray and Olivia

Mike and Gail Gurian

Jill Gibian and Mort Alexander

David and Lisa

Gordon and Ursula (Thanksgiving, 1990)

Rusty and Nancy Nelson and Paige Kenney

In January 1991, while Trina was in Spokane over Christmas and New Year's, we visited Nick, now a sophomore at the University of Washington. We had some bad weather on our return trip. Chains were required over Snoqualmie Pass. At one point our rear windshield cracked and shattered from the cold, leading to huge temperature differentials in front and back. But with Trina driving we made it home safely.

At the University Inn, January 1991

5

THE NEW ARRIVAL, 1991-1992

We devoted the spring and summer to what Olivia would call "nesting"— preparing the nest for our new arrival. We had already enclosed our yard with a chain-link fence when we got the dogs the year before. Now we enclosed the entire pasture as well. We put in an automatic sprinkler system in April, and then, to top it off, we installed a deck overlooking the river with a cascade of steps leading down to the river's edge. Sally had wisely planned a sabbatical leave in the spring quarter

Sally at our garden, summer 1991

On our new deck, 1991

Trina came in July 1991

Emmet Winkle von Stackelberg was born on Saturday, September 7th, 1991, at 1:40 p.m. after five hours of hard labor. He weighed 6 pounds, 7 ounces, and was 20 inches long.

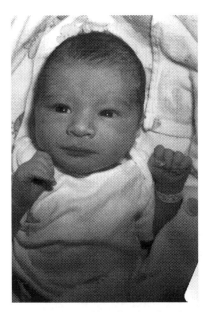

Emmet shortly after his birth

We named him after his great-great-great-great-granduncle Robert Temple Emmet, the Irish patriot and revolutionary who was executed at the age of twenty-five by the British in Dublin in 1803.

Monument to Robert Emmet on St Stephen's Green in Dublin

Emmet's birth was induced because Sally's doctors feared, groundlessly as it turned out, that he might not be getting enough nourishment in the womb. It left us feeling rather helpless in the face of high technology, which seemed to turn up more problems than it solved. Sally bore her labor with exemplary fortitude, refusing all anesthesia and rejecting her doctor's offer to do a Caesarian section to spare her further pain. Baby Emmet did fine throughout the pregnancy and birth, as attested by the high-tech devices that monitored his vital signs.

The birth was originally scheduled to be induced on September 6th. We got up at 5 a.m. to prepare to go to the hospital at 6 a.m. as instructed. However, due to several emergencies, the birthing center at Sacred Heart Medical Center could not receive Sally until late in the morning. Since she had requested a minimum of medical intervention, the doctors decided to induce labor by breaking her membranes. This proved impractical, however, due to the fact that her cervix was not yet sufficiently dilated. Because Emmet's heartbeat rose as a result of the medical intrusion, the doctors decided against using prostaglandin to dilate the cervix and opted for a slow dose of pitocin, which was administered intravenously all night from the 6th to the 7th.

At 8:30 Saturday morning Sally's membranes were broken, and she immediately went into hard labor. Within an hour her cervix had dilated to the maximum extent, and Emmet's birth seemed imminent. The nurses rushed the necessary utensils and receptacles for birth into the room. At the same time the head nurse decided to cut off the pitocin to slow down the contractions. This proved to be an unfortunate decision, as the contractions, while still painful, failed to move the baby down. For three hours there was very little movement, and the doctors and nurses were beginning to mention the dreaded word, C-section. Then, despite her exhaustion, Sally offered to change into a squatting position to facilitate the baby's movement. After one more hour of intense pushing, the delivery was accomplished, and Emmet gave his first cry to the relief and elation of his parents and birth helpers. An intensive care nurse stood by just in case the baby needed special attention. This proved to be unnecessary, however, as Emmet scored a nine for fitness on a scale of ten, missing a perfect score only because of some blue in hands and feet, which occurs quite normally in 90 per cent of all births. Emmet was born to the music of Chopin, which we had taped specially for the occasion. Throughout the day doctors and nurses making their rounds paused in the doorway to listen to the music. Dr. Busenholzer, the attending physician, paid us a big compliment: "What a lucky baby to have such parents!"

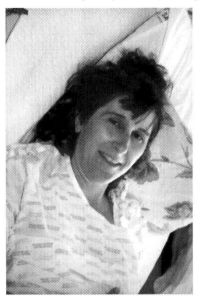

Exhausted, but happy

Emmet and his mother came home the following day, less than twenty-four hours after his birth. During the first two weeks he was a reasonably placid infant, though he suffered occasional bouts of colic. Sally nursed him every three or four hours. By the second week he was sleeping six hours a night. His grandparents, Amy and Carl Winkle, visited from September 15th through the 20th. His nineteen-year-old brother Nick, my son by my marriage to Steffi, was in Spokane from September 16th to 20th, before returning to the University of Washington in Seattle for his junior year in civil engineering. Emmet's twenty-five-year-old sister Trina lived in Cambridge and worked as an environmental risk assessment consultant.

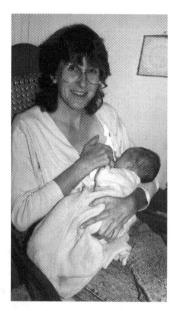

The new addition

Nick in his twentieth year

Emmet and his parents received numerous cards and presents from family and friends. Several friends had already visited Sally and Emmet in the hospital, including Lisa Brown, whose son Lucas would be born on February 28th the following year. Lisa spent the night before Emmet's birth at the hospital to keep Sally company, while I went home to tend the dogs and get some sleep. Other visitors were Olivia Caulliez, Ursula Hege, Gordon Gagliano, Nancy Nelson, Marion Dumoulin, and Tom and Esther Karier with their six-month-old son Marco. For many years Emmet would be part of a triumvirate of friends, separated by six months each from the older Marco and the younger Lucas. Mike and Gail Gurian and their baby daughter Gabrielle came after church on Sunday only to discover that we had already gone home!

The expanded family

Caption: On the deck, 1992

Winter clothing, knit by Mama

In the summer of 1982 we took our first trip abroad with the new infant. Before his twentieth birthday in September 2011, Emmet had been to Germany a full dozen times! In July 1992 we traveled to Baden-Baden, where Sally attended the annual conference of the American Association of Teachers of German (AATG).

Emmet, February 1992

Outfit from Ingrid, 1992

Emmet was a great hit at my father's home in Karlsruhe.

Emmet in Karlsruhe, July 1992

Im Rosengärtle with Halinka and Papa, 1992

On our return we visited Vermont in time to celebrate Olaf's sixtieth birthday, which also provided an occasion to celebrate Mama's 80th. We usually celebrated her January 20th birthday in the summer when the weather was more hospitable to family gatherings.

Mama at her eightieth birthday party, August 1992

Emmet, August 1992

Trina and Granny

Cousins Ginny and Kitty Biddle (More)

Nick Biddle, Joan, and daughters Barbara and Ginny

Olaf with Liz Biddle Barrett

Naomi and Matthew Shulman, August 1992

Emmet's first birthday, September 7, 1992

Never too young to read

6

ANOTHER YEAR, 1993-1994

1993 marked the end of my department chairmanship, and none too soon. I had become chair in 1987 when Betsy Downey, who seemed a permanent fixture in that position, suddenly decided she had had enough. She was having hot flashes, and the stress was getting to her. She designated me as her successor, and the department, now including Gena DeAragon, Tim Sarbaugh, and Steve Balzarini as well, duly followed her instructions and elected me to the position. My first three-year term went well, and I was reelected to a second term in 1990 with only one dissenting vote. My second term was not as successful. Betsy, in particular, took exception to my practice of hiring temporary adjuncts to teach Western Civilization with the authorization of the Dean of Arts and Sciences, Fr. Kevin Waters, but without consulting the department. Betsy led a departmental revolt against such high-handedness, and I would have resigned already in 1991 or 1992, if Fr. Schlatter had not persuaded me to at least serve out my term. This I reluctantly did, finally quitting in June 1993, to be replaced by Steve Balzarini. That fall I took my second sabbatical, this time for a full academic year.

Nick graduated from the University of Washington in June, 1993, with a degree in civil engineering and a specialization in wastewater management. He sought and got employment in Seattle, working for a number of environmental engineering firms over the years. Today he lives in Salt Lake City with his wife Kim Korinek, a professor of sociology at the University of Utah, and their son Sebi, born June 9th, 2010.

Nick's commencement at the University of Washington, June 12, 1993

Proud Dad, 1993

In August 1993 we went to Germany again, this time for the triennial Stackelberg family get-together at Schloss Höhnscheid. Trina and Nick attended as well and joined us in an excursion to the old university town of Marburg and several days in Berlin, the city where Trina was born.

Trina and Nick, 1993

Two of my nephews got married in 1993. Betsy's son Chris Chandler married Mireya at his rented summer home on Lake Willoughby in Vermont on August 21st.

Chris and Mireya's wedding with John Edmonds presiding and Julie and John as bridesmaid and best man, respectively

Betsy and her two daughters, August 1993

Sally with Mama, August 1993

Olaf's son John married Mariann at a beautiful winery in Kenwood, California, in November. This was also my first chance to get to know Trina's new boyfriend, Garth Jonson, a Canadian of Icelandic extraction a year behind Trina at Harvard. Garth had a quirky sense of humor that complemented Trina's own weakness for sarcasm very well. A year-and-a-half later they married in a private ceremony to which none of their relatives were invited.

John and Mariann's wedding, November 1993

Three brothers, older generation, 1993

Three brothers, younger generation (John Peter, and Paul), 1993

Earlier that year, in September, Sally's parents, Amy and Carl Winkle, celebrated their fiftieth wedding anniversary. They had married at the height of the Second World War, while Carl was on temporary leave.

Three sisters, Sally, Judy, and Sue, with Amy in the background, 1993

With Nick, September 1993

To cap off the year, we travelled to Toronto, Canada, to attend the annual convention of the Modern Language Association (MLA). The temperature was well below zero, very different from the last time I had been in Toronto, in May 1970, at the time of the Kent State shootings. This time we spent more time in Toronto's vast underground shopping complex with a hungry two-year-old in a futile search for an open restaurant. I was scheduled to give a paper on Ernst Nolte's (mis)interpretation of Nietzsche. Nolte, anxious to provide Nazism with an intellectual pedigree to rival Marxism (and at the same time to exonerate Christian conservatives from complicity with Nazism), portrayed Nietzsche as the philosophical progenitor of fascism. In my paper I refuted his charges point by point. I pointed out that Nietzsche had thoroughly condemned nationalism, antisemitism, and the militarism and imperialism of the Wilhelmine Monarchy and the Second Reich. He had clearly identified such contemporary leaders of the *völkisch* movement as the Imperial Court Pastor Adolf Stöcker and the racist Eugen Dühring as the foremost contemporary proponents of the "slave morality" he so despised. His "slave morality" was best exemplified by precisely the kind of world-rejecting "idealism" preached by the kind of *völkisch* ideologues whose right-wing counterparts would later support the Nazis. Although I thoroughly disagreed with Nolte on his interpretation of Nietzsche and shared none of his cold-war values, I was somewhat ambivalent about his very controversial role in the *Historikerstreit*. He had precipitated this "historians' dispute" by arguing that Nazism (and by extension the Holocaust) was just the mirror image of and an understandable reaction to the supposedly greater threat, violence, and criminality of "Asiatic" communism. This was an outrageous attempt to downplay Nazi atrocities, but I did appreciate Nolte's forthrightness in putting anti-Marxism (and its close relative, antisemitism) at the center of Nazi ideology.

> Nolte's analysis is superior to the liberals', whose values I nonetheless prefer: at least he views fascism as essentially different from communism, not as essentially the same. I despise Nolte's right-wing politics but I agree with his historical analysis. The value of Nolte's work lies in clearly showing the organic nature of Nazism: Nazism as an organic product of German society rather than an extraneous imposition. There's something honest about Nolte that appeals to me, no matter how much I may despise his political values.

While Nolte saw anti-communism as an at least partially redeeming trait of Nazism, I saw it as all the more reason to condemn Nazism! This was where our values were diagonally opposed. In February 1993 I wrote in my journal:

> The ultimate right-wing canard, which, if truly believed, attests almost to feeble-mindedness, is that egalitarians must believe that people have similar skills, talents, endowments, functions, etc. Egalitarians may be said to *contribute* to excellence by challenging the sense of entitlement of the "gifted," as if their gifts justify seizing the pie from the hungry.

Already in 1990, with the end of the cold war, I had noted:

> Why the Historikerstreit is *überholt* [no longer relevant]: the major force behind this right-wing revisionism was anti-communism. German history had to be revised to serve the anti-communist front (with U.S. blessing). For most of the historians in the dispute, exculpation of the Germans serves the anti-communist cause. Nolte is different, because for him the argument is reversed: anti-communism serves to revise (and upgrade) German history, not the other way around.

Ever since 1990 I had been following developments in Eastern Europe (the collapse of communism and the introduction, through "shock therapy," of capitalism) with dismay, as recorded in my journal over the years:

8/16/1990 The events of 1989 don't mean that Marxist analysis was wrong; they only mean that Marxist confidence was mistaken. Class analysis is not disproven by the fact that the bourgeoisie, the bourgeois spirit, has proven far stronger than Marx had expected.

8/18/1990 Communism serves a very useful function in Eastern Europe today, as the lightning rod that draws off social criticism and thus protects existing (or newly created) institutions and their privileged elites (mostly former communists). Perhaps that is the only way to introduce the free market: make communism take the blame for the hardships that will inevitably follow. That is the function of the Polish joke about communists having turned the aquarium into fish soup and free marketers facing the task of turning fish soup back into an aquarium.

The collapse of communism is revealing all sorts of truths: for one thing it reveals the time-honored Western assertion that the USSR is behind all world crises as the self-serving falsehood it always was.

The collapse of communism as the triumph of communist self-criticism. Is it too much to hope that it will lead to similar self-criticism in the West?

10/13/1990 The fascists' number one enemy has self-destructed.

12/18/1990 "Stability:" code word for protecting the privileged.

1/19/1991 The "Gulf War:" will it come to be seen as the first great North-South conflagration when the first world let the third world have it with all its technological superiority? The message to the impoverished masses of the world is, "Keep in your place." The hollowness of cold war rhetoric about Soviet expansionism now stands revealed. An imperialist power cannot help but behave like an imperialist power.

From the *American Historical Review* (Dec 1990), p. 1524: "The origins of the Dutch War provide another depressing illustration of the manner in which men of power are able to appropriate the consciences of men of talent."

4/13/1991 Is the lesson of the failure of communism that people are inevitably power-hungry, hence communism must degenerate into authoritarianism, or is it that human nature is indeed more resistant to change than optimists assumed, hence people cannot be won for a social order based on unselfishness?

4/27/1991 The easy transition of Stalinists to capitalists should throw into relief what is common to both: opposition to revolutionary democracy (Trotskyism).

5/27/1991 Memorial Day: the legalized murderers are celebrating their crimes.

6/20/1991 Project, not for me but for someone: show how the corruption of communism in the USSR is the result of timid, bureaucratic, Menshevik, bourgeois tradition, not of Leninist voluntarism. Perhaps it can't be done. Trotsky vs. Stalin.

6/29/1991 Two ways of looking at the collapse of communism: 1. Communism doesn't work; 2. Its enemies were too strong (the effort to sustain it was not great enough).

8/22/1991 The great political question of our time is, what is to prevent the property-owning majority from using its powers to protect its privileges? But even here there is historical progress. A hundred years ago the question would have read (world-wide at least) "the property-owning *minority.*" Multiculturalism as the political weapon of un-propertied minorities. Perhaps the failure of communism or Marxism is merely due to the shrinking of the underclass, i.e., to its success?? One more example of the dialectic.

Project: Socialism in the twentieth century: from the rise of the masses to the rise of elites. (Reflections on failed Soviet coup.) Coup leaders all referred to as right-wing conspirators. Good in showing that "left" still enjoys a more favorable aura. Even appropriate insofar as coup leaders were merely seeking to retain their power and privilege. Yet jarring to the extent that leaders acted on "true" socialist motives: the defense of equality and equity. And where the excluded are a minority socialism will not be "popular."

8/26/1991 Reflections on coup in USSR last week [in which coup leaders unsuccessfully tried to halt Gorbachev's reforms]: revolt of the new bourgeoisie in the USSR attests, in a sense, to the success of communism in creating a new bourgeoisie, who now feel thwarted by the system from achieving their full ambitions, including the ownership of private property. An ideology that originally gained appeal by promising freedom to the underclass, is now perceived as restricting the freedom of the dominant class. The contraction of the underclass and the growth of the dominant class, paradoxically made possible by communism, now account for its unpopularity.

1/10/92 Two aspects of the Cold War: on the one hand it was a campaign against communism as an authoritarian system; on the other hand it was a campaign in defense of the privilege of wealth against the militant advocates of the poor. As the century recedes, as communism collapses, the continuity of the North-South conflict becomes clearer.

The irony is that now [head of the German Democratic Republic Erich] Honecker is again to be punished for his communism: this time not by the Nazis, but by their heirs.

1/18/1992 Marxism is not dead; it is changing, developing, and growing. What *has* died are certain dogmas; what remains is the enterprise itself.

2/15/1992 Parallels in the "overthrow" of Christianity and communism: a rebellion against the imposition of virtue. People don't want to have to be charitable and love their neighbors. People don't want to be constrained in the pursuit of their own happiness. People want their own freedom, not others'. Rousseau (and Marx) were upset by this, which is why people are upset at them.

Maybe the advantage of Christianity over communism is that it can be practiced even if the whole world rejects it; not so communism, which can only be practiced under conditions that insure that everyone practices it.

2/22/1992 Why it is so necessary for the new Germany to punish Honecker: to create the illusion that the mass of common citizens were mere victims. Honecker's punishment makes possible the integration of East Germans in a united Germany.

2/23/1992 The Gulf War as defense of universal values of human rights—for Americans and Europeans: only through monopolization of fossil fuels at cheap prices can the material basis for the enjoyment of these rights be created. If Americans and Europeans were really interested in universalizing human rights, they would have to work for the redistribution of economic benefits that alone make the creation of the material basis for the enjoyment of human rights possible.

3/11/1992 Gena DeAragon's talk on feminist history entitled, "Add women and stir?" a formula she then criticized as insufficient. But in her response to questions she shows that she has herself not moved beyond this stage. When asked how she would write the history of the Gulf War from a feminist perspective, she said it should include the role of women in combat. Rather than critiquing the war itself as contrary to the interests of women, or of other groups excluded from power, she offered a "feminist" interpretation that not only leaves the patriarchal structure untouched but actually strengthens it.

3/15/1992 The great political question is, how do you develop true solidarity, true community? It is a question that challenges every community, from the family to the village to the nation to the human race. Socialism is a response to that challenge. Free market ideology is an avoidance mechanism. Fascism is deliberate deception.

9/5/1992 The vilification of Stalin as more criminal than Hitler is a function of our wealth and the need to defend it from the threatening poverty of the southern hemisphere. Hence the effort to impose equality must be seen as leading to greater crimes than the effort to maintain inequality... The effort to strengthen the underclass must be seen as more dangerous than the effort to strengthen the dominant class.

10/4/1992 The irony that now populations of former communist nations (e.g., East Germans) are considered to have a different mentality than people in the West—even though one argument against communism used to be that it presupposes the possibility (and desirability) of creating a "new person."

2/5/1994 Headline in the *New York Times* on the Chiapas rebellion: "Mexican Peasants Fighting the Future".

Emmet exhibited an early precociousness, as recorded in my journal:

2/22/1992 The study of little children as the study of human nature: Emmet starting to cry (out of impatience) just when Sally takes him on her lap and fiddles with her bra to expose her nipple to feed him—even though he may have shown no signs of hunger before. The prospect of immanent satisfaction making clear to him his state of dissatisfaction, which until then he had not noticed.

3/8/1992 Sally: "Roots and wings—I like that metaphor. That's what parents should give their children."

5/19/1992 Emmet, sitting behind me on the floor, laughing as I hit the computer keys, as if it were being done for his entertainment.

2/13/1993 End of the twentieth century: the first real word the baby says is "plane."

5/16/1993 Emmet's generic name for dogs, at least our two dogs, is "Marley." Having learned three names for two dogs, "Marley," "Cloudy," and "doggies," he is understandably confused as to which term refers to one of them or both.

5/28/1993 Emmet's first two phrases: "See you soon," and "I love you." Because he doesn't quite understand the second one, he gets them mixed up and usually says, "I love you soon." He can count to ten, but has no patience with seven or eight. On a good day he will get to six before jumping to nine and ten. On a bad day he jumps immediately from two to nine and ten!

2/5/1994 Emmet at 11 o'clock at night when I go in to put his blanket back on: "Hello, Daddy. I am sleeping. I don't want to wake up."

2/26/1994 Emmet: "Don't worry, Daddy. We all make mistakes." Or: "Just relax."

6/11/1994 Louise, after Emmet has successfully gone on the pot: "I'm so proud of you, Emmet." Emmet: "I'm proud of you, Louise."—Louise: "Why's that?"—Emmet: "Because you go on the potty."

7/7/1994 Emmet arriving at [Sally's colleague] Anna Monardo's party: "Hello. I'm Emmet. I'm two."

5/20/1995 Emmet saying not "When I grow up I'll be a daddy," but "When I grow up I'll be Daddy."

6/21/1995 Emmet: "When I grow up I'll be a belly dancer."

In 1992 our good friend and fellow Central America activist, Lisa Brown, decided to challenge the establishment head-on by running for the Washington state legislature. On October 18th, a couple of weeks before her victorious election, I recorded the following disagreement among her supporters:

The Lisa Brown campaign and the issue of Gail Ament's letter to the editor refuting an earlier letter-writer accusing Lisa of Marxism and sympathy for the Sandanistas [she had been in Nicaragua during the elections in 1990, in which the Sandanistas were defeated after blatant American intervention]: Gail's compelling defense of Lisa, including both an analysis of Nicaraguan society and a denunciation of efforts to distract attention from concrete Washington State issues, was criticized by Lisa and others for reviving an issue that should have been left dormant (on the assumption that people would forget about the earlier letter) and for giving "a rational response to an irrational attack." But that is just what the campaign *should* be doing! Their purely tactical concern with "winning" illustrates the process by which politics corrupts reasonable people.

Sally with Emmet and Lucas, 1993

Lisa and Lucas here for a visit, 1993

To our great delight Lisa won that election. She was also one of the few Democrats to be reelected in 1994, the year of the terrible Republican onslaught that led to the defeat of the incumbent Speaker of the national House of Representatives, Tom Foley. Lisa went on to a brilliant career as Majority Leader of the Washington State Senate.

I got some taste of local politics myself in the summer of 1993 when I was asked to represent land-owners on the Spokane River on a "Citizens' Advisory Commission" to the County Planning Department, which led to the following journal entry in August 1993:

> The complexity of politics. As a member of the Citizens' Advisory Committee to the County Planning Department I oppose on principle any measure that will lead to further development and higher residential density in rural areas. One way to prevent development is to oppose the extension of the sewer system, an absolute prerequisite for any major residential construction. But I favor sewer construction because it protects the drinking water. Yet extension of the sewer almost *requires* development—because of the huge financial cost. What position to take?

A couple of months later I recorded the following entry:

> Wayne Andresen, manager of the Inland Empire Paper Company, at the Citizens' Advisory Commission meeting yesterday, while speaking in opposition to the County Planning Department's policy of filing a formal title notice with the County Auditor on property that may be taken by the county to widen roadways or build new roads (the title notice serves as a way of officially informing property owners of the county's intention to take the property at its present value): "This is a question of what kind of society we want to live in, a society in which people are free to dispose of their property or a society in which property is controlled by the government."

On April 21ˢᵗ, 1994, Papa died, a month short of his 84ᵗʰ birthday. It was the first of a series of deaths to come in the years that followed, involving not only our parents' generation, but our own and our children's generations as well. Papa's death did not receive much notice in the German press, overshadowed as it was by the death, on the same day, of former U.S. President Richard Nixon.

7

ENDINGS AND BEGINNINGS, 1994-1995

All eight of his children (by two marriages) attended Papa' funeral in April 1994, turning it into the kind of bibulous wake he himself would have enjoyed. The ceremony itself was in a packed church, the largest in Karlsruhe, with mourners and gawkers crowding the sidewalks outside. His body was then transported to the cemetery in the Bavarian town of Bad Reichenhall, where he was buried next to his parents. Here in Reichenhall his journey had begun in his pre-teenage years after the expulsion of his family from their ancestral home in Estonia in 1919.

Papa's grave in Bad Reichenhall, April 1994

On our way back from Reichenhall to Karlsruhe we made an *Abstecher* (side-trip) to some of our old haunts during the war, specifically to the Elmhof, Neubeuern, and Hinterhör. The latter had changed dramatically from the way we remembered it. Once the bustling country estate of my godmother, the Countess Degenfeld, "Sweety" to us, it now seemed deserted and moribund. In contrast, the Elmhof was in ship-shape condition, unchanged from the way we remembered it, but with a new coat of paint.

Hinterhör, 1994

In the summer of 1994, Emmet's grandparents, Amy and Carl Winkle, came to Spokane for their annual visit. This time we decided to take a trip to Penticton, Canada, a very pleasant drive in Carl's air-conditioned Cadillac. However, the destination was ill-chosen. Penticton, a beautiful town with two picturesque lakes, was enveloped in a haze of smoke generated by a fire raging in the forested hillside at the edge of town. We were lucky to find motel rooms, as a bit later in the day all rooms were taken by residents of the hillside homes consumed in or endangered by the fire. Two-year-old Emmet was fascinated by the fire-fighting planes that dipped low into the lake to scoop up water to pour on the flames. Emmet himself was allowed to go into the water only up to his waist, however. The day before, he had suffered some burns backing into our grill. We had to take him to the emergency room for treatment of his burns.

Grandpa and Grandma Winkle, summer 1994

Summer 1994

Louise and Jack Dolan, summer 1994

In September 1994 my "godson" Johnnie Van Duyl came to visit us over Labor Day. We attended the Spokane Symphony's free concert in Comstock Park with my colleague Tim Sarbaugh and his family. Our animated conversation drew an admonition from a neighboring couple to please lower our voices.

Johnnie Van Duyl, Labor Day weekend, 1994

Sarah and Tim Sarbaugh with Mary Catherine and Chris, 1994

Emmet started pre-school at the YMCA in September 1994. He would certainly have been ready for school much sooner than 1998, when he started first grade, but we held him back (in compliance with the Washington state law establishing six as the age of school entry). While he was intellectually ready for school a year earlier, we thought he would benefit socially by being one of the older students in his class. Having graduated from high school at barely seventeen, I learned from my own example, but also from my son Nick's experience, who graduated at seventeen as well, not yet having achieved his full growth.

School picture 1994

Spring 1995

In May 1995 I celebrated my sixtieth birthday. Sally and I went out to dinner at one of our favorite restaurants, the Mustard Seed. Looking out the window, I was surprised to see Nick in the parking lot. What a surprise, I thought; he must have guessed we would be here. Of course it had all been prearranged by Sally, but the thought never occurred to me.

Nick in Vermont, Christmas 1994

Mama at Steffi's for Christmas, 1994

In the summer of 1995 Sally attended a six-week seminar on film at the University of Rhode Island. Emmet and I joined her in Providence in July. We visited my cousin Johnny Edmonds, an Episcopalian priest in Newport, before heading up to Vermont to see Mama.

Newport. RI, summer 1995

Mama, August 1995

Vermont. August 1995

Tea for Trina and Garth at Buzzy and Steffi's, August 1995

For Emmet's fourth birthday on September 7th we were back in Spokane.

Emmet on his fourth birthday, September 1995

Emmet, Lucas, and Lisa, September 1995

8

Early Deaths, but Life Goes On, 1996-1997

It began with the premature death of my former Harvard roommate Paul Russell of pancreatic cancer at the age of sixty-one on February 14th, 1996. I had spoken to him on the phone the summer before, when we were in Rhode Island, and we were looking forward to a visit. A few days before the scheduled visit Deborah called to say Paul was indisposed and wished to cancel the visit. He had just received his lethal diagnosis and was in no mood to see me. I wondered to what degree his unwillingness to see me was my own fault.

> Can I put my finger on the problem of my relationship with Paul? I appreciated him more than anyone else, but that may have been the problem. Our relationship may have been structured in a way that forced him to play a role toward me—always interested, always in good humor, always ready to treat or to help me. I always had the vague feeling that I'm somehow corrupting him, reducing his ability to function in the conventional world, aestheticizing him. I imagined that his family viewed my influence with skepticism, if not suspicion. One proof was his father's admonition to Paul: "Why do you talk so fast?"

> Even when Paul admitted a weakness, showed a weakness, displayed, ever so faintly, a need, or uttered, ever so softly, a call for help, it always seemed he did so to help me, to make me feel I was not alone or off base in my need for help.

I learnt more from Paul than from all my professors put together.

I did not see Paul again before his death. I felt sure he did not want me to see him in his deteriorating condition, although maybe that was only a pretext for me to stay away. In my get-well cards I kept up a false optimism, usually closing with pro-forma phrases like, "Hope to see you next summer." Deborah asked me to give a eulogy at Paul's memorial service in Harvard's Memorial Church. This is what I said:

> I am a voice out of Paul's youth. We first met as callow freshmen 44 years ago in Weld Hall, right here across the Yard. We roomed together in Adams House and remained good friends after college, despite the fact that we usually lived thousands of miles apart. Friendship with Paul was my most memorable and lasting experience at Harvard. I'd like to share with you an entry in my journal on August 19, 1955, after a visit to the Russell farm in Turner, Maine:
>
>> Paul's sociability, consideration, and intelligent conversation make him very enjoyable company. His main asset is an un-ebbing interest and openness—he is the perfect listener—he is interested in almost everything that is said, and he doesn't either overwhelm with talk or sit silently. He is the kind of person out of whom you get proportionately as much as you put in. That is, you can disregard him, and say only a few pleasantries, and you will get a few pleasantries in return. Or you can sit and chatter to him about yourself, and you will get a receptive audience. Or you can probe deeper, and inquiringly discuss, deal with a problem or topic with all the resolution you can muster, and you will be sure to get an equal effort, which usually produces a superior result, from Paul. That is why it is always satisfying and usually rewarding to talk to Paul.
>
> In my family we always agreed, Paul was a born psychiatrist. It was as if the training he received was superfluous, the substance was what counted and that was always there. He had the helping and comforting disposition. I was always the hypochondriac who went to him for sustenance and medical advice. He was an unfailing source of encouragement and

strength. We complemented each other in more ways than one. He introduced me to philosophy, I introduced him to music. Both of us preferred our intellectual and aesthetic interests to our formal courses. Which sometimes meant we had to cram for exams. I'll never forget Paul reading Immanuel Kant's <u>Critique of Pure Reason</u> in one night. I found him in his armchair in the morning, transfigured. "John [the name by which I was known at Harvard]," he said, "last night I saw the truth."

Paul always reminded me of that great Tolstoyan character, Pierre, in <u>War and Peace</u>, or perhaps it was Pierre that reminded me of Paul. They had a very similar, slightly eccentric, but ultimately unique mix of generosity, intellect, and humor. I thought Henry Fonda was totally miscast in the film, much too smooth and conventional. It really should have been Paul. Didn't they understand Tolstoy? But maybe one couldn't understand or appreciate the character that Tolstoy was trying to create . . . unless one knew Paul.

Paul's memorial service was the first "funeral" my twenty-nine year-old daughter Trina, who accompanied me, had ever attended. In my eulogy, somewhat spatially confused, I had pointed in the opposite direction from Weld Hall, leading Trina to question me later in an admonitory tone, "Are you sure you really went to Harvard?"

On May 24th it was the turn of my forty-three year-old colleague Tim Sarbaugh to die of cancer. Tim had been struggling with his health all winter and was even hospitalized briefly, but his cancer wasn't diagnosed until a week or two before his death when he collapsed on his way to a medical examination. This perseverance and refusal to neglect his duties was typical of Tim, easily the most popular and conscientious teacher in the department and probably the university as a whole. Every day during the noon hour, when I was reclining in my easy chair to get some rest between classes, I heard students coming and going in his office next door. His door was always open! His students loved his attentiveness and eagerly sought his advice. His classes were always oversubscribed. His dynamism was contagious. To me it seemed he was a man in a hurry. Betsy Downey's nickname for him was, "Tigger." His much-too-early death seemed to explain why he was so driven.

The most tragic death of all occurred on my sixty-second birthday, May 8th, 1997. Olaf's son Peter died unexpectedly of a heart attack in his thirty-eighth year. He had been quite ill shortly before, but seemed to have recovered when tragedy struck. It has forever marred the celebration of my birthday, which henceforth seemed inextricably linked to my nephew's death.

Peter, his wife Nancy, and her two daughters Megan and Kirsten

Peter at the grill, 1996

The most violent of the early deaths occurred in November 1997. My half brother, Curt, Jr., known in the family as "Bubi" (boy), snapped in a moment of despair. Deeply in debt and facing criminal charges for financial wrongdoing in investments in the former East German Democratic Republic, he decided not only to commit suicide, but also, in what can only be explained as temporary insanity, to take his wife Allusch and their two young sons with him. He shot them and himself with his *Bundeswehr* (federal army) revolver, which he had kept after his obligatory one-year military service. He tried to cover up his deed by setting his house on fire. His sisters were sure that Bubi and his family had been victims of an outside attack, perhaps by others implicated in his financial misdeeds, but the police determined that there had been no forced entry into the house. Olaf was the only member of the American side of the family to attend his very sad funeral in Germany at the end of November.

With Bubi (b. 1956) in the Rosengärtle, 1960

In the summer of 1996 we again went to Germany for the triennial Stackelberg *Familientag*, spending several days in Berlin and also visiting the picturesque city of Lübeck, where Sally was slated to begin teaching in Eastern Washington University's summer abroad program the following year.

**At Eva and Günther's, with their daughter Elena
and granddaughter Noema, 1996**

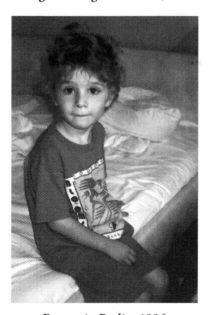

Emmet in Berlin, 1996

Professionally, the academic year 1996-1997 was surprisingly productive. Fr. Schlatter entered partial retirement in 1997, leaving the Robert K. and Ann J. Powers Chair in the Humanities vacant. Given my strained relations with some of my history department colleagues and the fact that the Chair was open to members of the English and philosophy departments as well, I viewed my chances of succeeding Fr. Schlatter as very slim indeed. Most unexpectedly, however, my application was approved by the committee convened by the dean, Fr. Michael McFarland, to select Fr. Schlatter's successor. Undoubtedly a glowing letter of recommendation written by my increasingly well-known colleague at Pacific Lutheran University, the Holocaust scholar Chris Browning, played an important role in my selection. This meant a considerable boost in salary, and, more importantly, a handsome travel budget as well. I used those extra funds to attend the annual American Historical Association (AHA) conference at the end of the year, giving me the chance to personally contact various publishers and obtain the most favorable contract for my book, eventually titled, *Hitler's Germany: Origins, Interpretations, Legacies*. I chose Routledge, a respected world-wide publisher of scholarly books, which brought out the book the following year, in spring 1999.

On the subject of academic scholarship, I recorded the following thoughts in January 1997:

> The kind of thing that "makes my day" these days: discovering in the writings of someone I respect some evidence—or even just a hint—that they have read something I have written, that they have taken to heart a point I have made. Example: Alan Steinweis writing that he is more concerned about mainstream diffusion of books like *The Bell Curve* than about marginal Holocaust denial on the Northwestern University website. It not only suggested to me that he had read my review of Kühnl's book on the links between American eugenicists (geneticists) and Nazism; it also showed that he agreed with my positive evaluation of the book (as against the critical review in the AHR [*American Historical Review*] which linked Kühnl's book with Nolte's revisionism). It works negatively, too, of course: the depressing feeling on reading [David] Blackbourn's dismissal of "vulgarized idealism" as a source of Nazism in the *London Review of Books*.

Meanwhile Emmet was continuing to grow up, as recorded in my journal:

> 4/8/96 Emmet saying he wants to go to Gonzaga when he grows up! Where did he get that? In stark contrast to Trina and Nick.

4/10/96 Emmet, overheard at pre-Kin, speaking to some classmates: "My dad is sixty million years old. That's quite amazing. Imagine that!"

5/18/96 Emmet, upon hearing that Dole was running for president: "Is he going to wear shorts?"

5/27/96 Emmet, playing basketball with Louise, after Louise makes a shot: "Way to go, baby!"

2/12/97 Emmet, disappointed that Sally had to pour back some of the good-tasting medicine into the bottle, thus delaying his enjoyment: "Oh no, I was in the middle of my excitement."

6/2/97 Neighbor Butch extolling Emmet: "He's so smart, but he still has common sense."

8/20/97 Emmet, to whom I pointed out a "school" of small fish down by the river: "It looks like they're on a field trip."

12/6/97 Emmet: "I'm just like you, Dad. I don't like to speak on the telephone, either."

1/7/98 Emmet's Sally-expressions: "Don't you understand?" "Didn't you know that?" "Seek and you shall find."

Impressed by the belly-dancers he watched on our occasional visits to Azar's, an excellent Mid-Eastern restaurant in Spokane, Emmet said that he hoped to become a belly-dancer when he grew up.

Emmet belly-dancing, 1997

My two sons, 1995

Volksfest in Berlin with Ingrid and Trina

With Sylvie, Wolfi, Halinka and Patrik, 1996

Trina, Nick, and Emmet at the *Familientag*, 1996

Heinrich and Trina tapping beer, 1996

***Familientag* 1996**

My political entries continued to reflect my disenchantment with the nation's growing rightward trend, only briefly slowed by Clinton's reelection in 1996.

4/24/94 The dialectic: today it is politically correct to oppose "political correctness." It is politically correct to see its dangers everywhere. It is politically correct to condemn pressures to be politically correct.

4/7 95 Variation on the proverb, "Hypocrisy is the homage that vice pays to virtue:" The charge of political correctness is the homage that conservatives pay to progressivism.

7/26/95 American fascism: a fundamental stacking of the deck by the strong for the strong.

1/5/96 My book [the as yet unpublished *Hitler's Germany*]: not just a history of specifically European fascism, but a case study of how fascistic ideas and practices come about. The hope is that, *mutatis mutandis*, it will help people understand American fascism, even though it may be quite different in appearance from its European precursor.

3/12/96 The only reason "left" and "right" today have "no meaning" is because the left is weak—there is no labor movement, no organized class struggle. The right triumphant has a vested interest in getting rid of the notion of "left," traditionally associated with positive values—humanitarianism, progress, etc.—so that the right can lay claim to these values, while evading any challenge from the left. Getting rid of the left-right distinction allows the right to claim to be the mainstream—and insofar as that claim is or seems to be justified, the left-right distinction does seem increasingly irrelevant, even impertinent, as if there is or even can be an equal "political force" on the other (non-right) side. The only consolation is that the "right" has absorbed much of the program of the "left," without acknowledgement, or even awareness. But that is ever how progress has been made.

5/9/96 Insofar as the environmental issue has become the central issue of our time, displacing the issue of economic distribution, there are some grounds for asserting that the left-right model is no longer relevant. On the other hand, there are still left- and right-wing approaches to solving this and other problems—based on how the proposed solution contributes to the commonweal. The issue of equality will still distinguish left- from right-wing policies.

6/9/96 socialism and freedom: freedom only exists where there is a possibility of choices. Freedom may be restricted under socialism, but it is nonsense to say that it exists—or is available to most people—under capitalism.

9/1/96 Basic to any progressive worldview is the notion that humans make their own history and can control their own destiny.

6/29/97 The lie and the vice at the heart of anti-communism—that their opposition is opposition to dictatorship rather than to egalitarianism. For them the plight of the poor is simply not an issue worth rearranging society or even worth worrying about.

7/3/97 The wealthy and successful need to remember that they are the beneficiaries of a system that also seems to require poverty and failure.

7/11/97 Scandalous thoughts: if fascism comes to America , it will be in the Republican Party.

9/7/97 The assumption in all the literature is that cooperation with the STASI (*Staatssicherheitsdienst* [state security service]) is reprehensible in itself. Informing is always evil. It must have been motivated by pure self-interest, to obtain advantages for oneself by collaborating with authority. My interpretation is different: There must have been people like me who were committed to socialism but only too aware of the extraordinary and intense opposition it faced from "moneyed" interests. Collaborating in a socialist project meant defending it from its ubiquitous, determined enemies—determined to thwart it. If covert action is permissible for the defense of liberal democracy, why should it be impermissible for the defense of socialism? If even the strong feel entitled to resort to such devices in defense of their vision of a good society, why should they be illegitimate for the advocates of the weak? If covert action is defensible for majorities, why should it be indefensible for minorities—who have much better reason to resort to it, because they have far fewer "legitimate" means to insure the survival of their project and vision?

My niece Naomi Shulman married her fiancé Chris Templin in a beautiful wedding in Essex Junction, on the west side of the state of Vermont, in the summer of 1997.

Naomi and Chris Templin, June 1997

Alvin, Marty, and Carol Shulman, June 1997

Mama and Matt Shulman, June 1997

Mama and Sally, June 1997

Mother and daughter, June 1997

Brother and sister, June 1997

Mama at Tempy's, summer 1997

On September 7th, we celebrated Emmet's sixth birthday.

Emmet's sixth birthday, September 1997

Emmet, summer 1997

With Johnnie and his friend Norman Pate, 1997

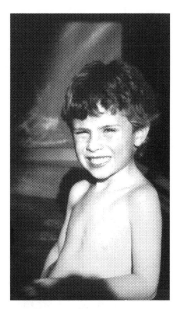

Emmet in our new hot tub, 1997

Emmet's new puppet theatre, 1997

9

THE END OF AN ERA, 1998

Mama died on December 22nd, a month short of her eighty-seventh birthday. We never did find out the specific cause (according to our physician cousin Ginny, it may have been stomach cancer). Mama did finally, after much family pressure, consent to go to the hospital, but only long enough to be treated for dehydration. For all practical purposes she stopped eating sometime in the fall and wasted away, reduced to skin and bones by the time of her death. Olaf knew that something was badly wrong when Mama refused even a bite from one of Cora's home-baked muffins, which she usually devoured with relish. She was determined to die at home in her bed with a minimum of medical intervention, and that's what she did. She showed us how to die.

Although Mama had been looking forward to the long-planned Emmet family get-together in Ireland in June in commemoration of the 200th anniversary of the failed uprising against the British in 1798, when the time came she was too weak to go. Olaf delivered the verdict, "For her the trip comes too late." I saw her for the last time in July 1998 on our return from Ireland and our brief follow-on trip to Germany. Sally remained in Germany to teach a summer course at the *Fachhochschule* [university of applied science] in Lübeck, still one of Spokane's sister cities at the time. Parting from his mother was quite traumatic for six-year-old Emmet who cried bitterly as his mother waved good-bye from the station platform. Later, back in Spokane, he bravely told her over the phone, "I'm getting over my fear of missing you." I recorded some impressions from our visit to Mama in my journal in July 1998:

Insights from my visit to Vermont. Two paradigmatic clashes between Betsy and Mama in which, despite my overall condemnation of how Mama has treated Betsy over the years, I found myself far more in agreement with Mama: one was Betsy's typically clumsy (and condescending) attempt to be "nice" to Mama by telling Emmet that the presents she had bought for him also came from Mama. "I can give my own gifts, thank you," was Mama's predictable response. The second clash came after Emmet described how Louise had yelled at her daughter Sherry and told her to "get out of here." Mama rebuked Emmet for revealing this embarrassing family dispute. This provoked Betsy into rising to Emmet's defense. "I think it's perfectly all right for him to talk about it. Do you want him to lie?" It was only after I twice defended Mama's censure as perfectly appropriate that Betsy gradually gave in.

I managed to deflect most direct clashes of my own with Mama, two of which stick out in my mind. One was over the remark I made when Emmet was chasing after Mama's half-wild kittens who always fled at his approach. In a facetious tone I said, "He likes to feel the power," and was most displeased when Mama took the remark so seriously. "Oh no. That's so wrong. That view is imposed on children by grown-ups. Children want to get close to animals." Her contorted face showed how strongly she felt about this, as if she had struck at the source of our civilizational malaise. I did not feel that it was worth it to try to explain that I had meant my remark facetiously. Advice to visitors to Mama: know when *not* to make small talk.

The other run-in came on the subject of Berlin. I knew that she had not liked Berlin when she lived there (her marriage was dissolving), so I did not want to give her occasion to contradict me by expressing a positive judgment. Deliberately non-committal, I said, "Berlin has really changed." Predictably, however, that did not stop her at all. "I detest Berlin. It's an awful, narrow-minded, self-important city."

I did not think this was the last time I would see Mama, although she tried to persuade me to stay longer, saying that maybe next year at this time she might no longer be alive. I told her we had to get back to tend to our dogs, an argument she found difficult to counter, since all her life she had used the same excuse to justify not budging from her place.

Mama on the deck of her home in Vermont, July 1998

Mama in the sun, July 1998

Mama indoors, July 1998

With Trina and Mama, July 1998

After returning from Vermont, I reflected on what turned out to be (although I did not yet know it) our final parting.

The peculiar implications of Mama's mumbled "you're a good boy" at our parting in Vermont. It was quite unexpected—and unpleasant—to me. For one thing, expressing a "judgment" like that suggested that she was not at all emotionally involved (at the brink of tears, for instance) by our going away. For another thing, it was said in a way that seemed to refute a previously held conviction (such as that I was *not* a good boy). Even the way it was said, hardly audible, seemed to suggest that she was talking to herself, revising an earlier opinion. Or if it was said to me, as it must have been given the pronoun "you," it singularly lacked conviction. Aside from the fact that the whole phrase was rather patronizing to begin with, suggesting that its main aim was simply to once again establish the mother-son relationship (like straightening my tie years ago, or asking me to run a trivial errand, to which Aunt Temple had objected almost thirty years ago.)

Mama was not defeated by old age. She told Maureen Dyer, "I can't see anything, I can't hear anything, and I can't remember anything, and I've never been so happy in my life." Maureen told Mama about her own mother's Alzheimer's. "She's in a nursing home, but for all she knows about it, she could just as well be in Hoboken." Mama: "How awful! I'd much rather be in Hoboken and think I was in a nursing home." Mama gave us instructions for her funeral. "I want all four of you to get drunk. I want my body cremated and the ashes thrown out on the dump behind the house." At the time of her death, three of her children were over sixty years of age and the fourth one turned sixty the following day.

12/22/1998 Mama's death. Notified by Trina by phone at 5 a.m.(Ruth Lawrence had phoned her mother) shortly after I had woken from a remarkable dream of Mama, thin, even skeletal, but active and moving, on her farm, which was, however, more abundant and comfortable than in reality. What made the dream extraordinary was that residing as a rather unwanted guest on the outskirts of her property were Hitler and a number of his aides, all rather ridiculous as they had no power, which also made them seem uncharacteristically moderate, since their words were empty threats (a reflection, perhaps, of my dismissal in class of the Aryan Nation as too insignificant to be the quintessential form of American fascism—it was the Ku Klux Klan that I had hoped to elicit from my students). Hitler's minions dutifully went to pick up their grub at the main house, so many tamed monsters.

The pain of Mama's death lies in the sudden realization of all those missed years when I barely saw her or talked to her, as if they would never end. I truly took her for granted. The pain of knowing at the end of her life how lonely she was. Although I never saw her more than once a year for the past twenty years, her death pulls the ground from under me. Her death also takes much of the pleasure from writing my book [*Hitler's Germany*]. I now realize how much I was writing it for her.

As Mama had predicted, her funeral provided the first occasion in years for her four children, now all over sixty years in age, to gather together in one place. It seemed to me that Olaf, who inherited the role of "top dog" in the family, unconsciously adopted many of Mama's mannerisms. But he was critical of her ready acceptance of violence and predation in the natural world. Mama understood that her love of nature was a corollary to her dislike of human society. "I'm anti-social," she once told me; "I love living at the end of the world." As the second-oldest living Emmet (among the more than four-hundred living direct descendants of Thomas Addis Emmet—the founding father of the American branch of the Emmet family), Mama would have loved to attend the week-long family reunion in Ireland in June 1998. It was indeed a most enjoyable celebration, well-organized by our cousins, Susanna Doyle, Grenville ("Jeremy") Emmet, and Katie Emmet.

Three brothers in Ireland

Abbey Tavern, Howth, June 26, 1998

In Ireland, June 1998

Robert Emmet's statue on St Stephen's Green, Dublin

At the Temple Bar Hotel, Dublin

Trina, Nick, Xuiwei, and Olaf in Ireland

Eva and Günther, 1998

Emmet in Ireland, 1998

Emmet finished Kindergarten and entered first grade shortly before his seventh birthday in September 1998.

Emmet's seventh birthday, 1998

His Kindergarten teacher Linda Lentz gave him a glowing report:

Emmet expresses himself well and can easily talk to both children and adults. He enjoys interacting with literature and is eager to answer questions and join in group discussions. Emmet is well-liked by all his classmates. He uses words to handle conflicts that arise. Even though he chooses to spend much of his time with Lucas [Brown], he is able to easily work and play with any of the other children.

Emmet enjoys success in using scissors, pencils, paint, glue, etc. He is printing his name nicely using lower-case letters. He works hard to do quality work. One of Emmet's favorite free time activities is to build a stage using blocks and sing and "play" his block guitar. He also enjoys the computers. Emmet is a good listener during circle. We enjoy him immensely.

On a much higher level Trina was also adding to her academic achievements.

Trina getting her MS degree at the Harvard School of Public Health, 1998

1998 was the year of President Bill Clinton's impeachment (and eventual acquittal) for having lied when he denied having had sexual relations with White House intern Monica Lewinsky, based on Clinton's dubious claim that oral sex did not constitute sexual relations. My view was that while Clinton's actions may have been morally reprehensible and politically misguided, they did not constitute sufficient grounds for impeachment. The exploitation of the case by Republicans for political advantage seemed to me to outweigh Clinton's misdeeds. I noted a resemblance between the prosecution of Clinton and the prosecution of informers in the former East Germany.

> [Joachim] Gauck, the man in charge of investigation of the [former] East German STASI (the state security service), reminds me of Kenneth Starr, special prosecutors. Both men have grown into their jobs to such an extent that they can't seem to face any other employment. Both have developed elaborate, passionate rationales for the importance, indeed the necessity, of their jobs. In both men one gets the impression that their jobs have affected all their attitudes, indeed their personalities. Their self-serving motives are so obvious as to make it very difficult to take seriously their vilification of the objects of their investigations. If

they weren't right-wingers before, they would have to become right-wingers now. Thus does the material base determine the superstructure of values and ideas with unusual directness. Rarely do we have such unmediated examples of economic determinism.

The other big event of 1998 was Ursula and Gordon's wedding.

Ursula and Gordon's wedding at Patsy Clark's

The Women's Group at Ursula's wedding

The men of the women's group, 1998

Epilogue

The years after 1999 were marked by a gradual, but unmistakable decline in energy, health, and eventually productivity. These were also the terrible years of the George W. Bush presidency and its associated horrors, many of them continued in the Obama administration, despite the unrealistic hopes vested in his election in 2008. My book, *Hitler's Germany: Origins, Interpretations, Legacies*, was published by Routledge in 1999. In 2002 Sally and I collaborated on *The Nazi Germany Sourcebook: An Anthology of Documents*, and after my retirement from teaching in 2004, I completed my "Nazi trilogy" with a reference work, *The Routledge Companion to Nazi Germany* (2008). Punctuating this minor surge of productivity were back surgery in 1999, a radical prostatectomy in 2005, and sinus surgery in 2010. My physical decline reached a preliminary climax with a stroke in July 2011, leaving my left side paralyzed. I no longer have the desire nor the energy to chronicle this stage of my life in detail, though I may intermittently continue my memoirs on my website at www.roderickstackelberg.com. It is now time for the younger generations to carry the torch for a better world. May they be more successful than we were.